Essential Documents
Environment

THE COMPLEMENTARY WEBSITE

The http://books.indicator.co.uk website gives you instant access to all the ready-to-use documents, tools, policies, etc. that complement this publication.

Go to

http://books.indicator.co.uk

and enter your access code
RPK754

THE CD-ROM

Don't have access to the Internet?
Call Customer Services on 01233 653500 to request a CD-ROM.

Cover: ©iStockphoto.com

ISBN 978-1-906892-32-6

Second Edition - First print - E02P1

Introduction

The environment is a difficult subject to stay on top of at the best of times. And it's not just the legislation you have to worry about. With the growing number of companies adopting corporate social responsibilty policies and ISO environment management systems, the demands on your business are increasing. You're being asked for policies, procedures etc. and are expected to minimise your environmental impacts wherever possible. Added to this is the ever-present threat of enforcement action if you get it wrong. However, it's not all negative, as good environmental techniques can also save you money; most notably through reducing your energy use and the amount of waste you have to pay to be disposed of.

For this reason, we decided to produce **Essential Documents: Environment**. It includes policies, checklists, guidance notes and forms, which you can use either to help you achieve compliance or satisfy the requirements of a potential customer. It's divided into ten chapters which cover everything from waste management through to recycling and energy saving. Each chapter is accompanied by a useful commentary that describes how each document should be used. And with the complementary **Download Zone** website you can copy, adapt and print each one to suit your personal needs.

Ideally this book should become a useful companion to help you stay legally compliant, reduce your overheads and satisfy any commercial requirements. If you'd like to see other documents added, please contact us and we'll endeavour to include them in future editions.

Simon Wakeham CMIOSH
Editor-in-Chief

March 2011

Contents

Chapter 1

Environmental incidents

Environmental incident investigation
policy and procedure

Although no business sets out to cause accidental pollution, unfortunately, it happens all too often. So if you suspect that you've allowed a substance to pollute, you need to find the source, identify how it was able to pollute and take steps to prevent a reoccurrence.

LEGAL POSITION

The principal legislation concerning the control of environmental incidents and pollution prevention is the **Environmental Protection Act 1990** and the **Pollution Prevention and Control Act 1999**. In addition to identifying the procedures and licensing requirements for discharges, emissions and waste disposal, the Acts outline the requirements for integrated pollution and prevention and the principle of "the polluter pays". Therefore, failing to comply with the requirements of the Acts and allowing an environmental or pollution incident to occur could result in your organisation paying large fines and footing the bill for the cost of the clean up.

INVESTIGATION OF ENVIRONMENTAL INCIDENTS

If you are unfortunate enough to suffer an environmental incident, you need to know what action to take. To help you and your staff take the correct action, why not use our **Environmental Incident Investigation Policy and Procedure**. Our document outlines what constitutes an environmental incident, how your business can manage it, and how to minimise the potential environmental impact. As with any policy, you need to ensure that you comply with it; the enforcement agencies will always evaluate what you have actually done, against what you say you will do in the policy.

ENVIRONMENTAL INCIDENT INVESTIGATION POLICY AND PROCEDURE

1. General statement

It is our policy that all identified environmental incidents will be recorded and investigated. In the first instance an Environmental Incident Report will be completed as soon as an incident has been identified. Witness Statement Records are also to be prepared where applicable.

The purpose of this policy is to show that we take our environmental management responsibilities seriously and that the causes and consequences of all such incidents can be established. Systems and procedures can then be established to prevent them from recurring. Therefore, all staff are expected to abide by the following procedures and cooperate with management in the event of an incident.

2. Legal position

The law concerning environmental incidents is principally covered by:

- the **Environmental Protection Act 1990**

Not all incidents need to be reported, however environmental incidents involving damage or danger to the natural environment, pollution, risks to wildlife, spills of hazardous waste should all be reported in the first instance to the Environment Agency. **The emergency number is 0800 807060 24 hours a day**.

3. Definitions

Environmental incident - the release, either accidental or malicious, of a harmful substance. For example:

- chemical or oil spillage
- accidental release of a harmful chemical to the atmosphere
- accidental release of a harmful substance to the drainage/sewerage system
- accidental release of a harmful substance to a local watercourse.

Major incident - an incident requiring the involvement of a regulatory authority due to the volume or toxicity of the harmful substance released.

Minor incident - an incident not requiring the involvement of a regulatory authority.

4. Reasons for investigating

The following reasons will be considered during investigations of reported incidents:

- to ensure that the causes of a particular incident have been rectified
- to ensure that the preventive measures implemented are adequate
- to determine whether any specific breaches of legislation have occurred
- to increase the company's knowledge and awareness
- to demonstrate to the enforcement agencies that the incident has been taken seriously.

5. Investigation of incidents

All incidents are to be investigated as soon after the event as possible. This should ideally be carried out by a responsible person who is familiar with the site and the processes involved. An Environmental Incident Report is to be prepared to record the facts of the incident. This will also detail any immediate actions that have been taken to mitigate/rectify the situation and any further action which may also be required as a result of the incident.

The Environmental Incident Report should also be supported by photographs and sketches of the incident.

Witness Statements should also be completed by any person involved in the incident, any witnesses to the incident and by those responsible for reporting the incident.

Where appropriate, samples of any substances, including the substance released, soil samples and polluted water samples, should be obtained in order to assess the toxicity and potential effects on the wider environment. Depending upon the nature of the substance, the appropriate personal protective equipment must be used.

Following the collation of the above information and the preparation of an incident report form, a review of the incident and the circumstances surrounding it should be implemented by the company's senior management to ensure that the appropriate lessons have been learned, and that all necessary control measures and staff training have been implemented to prevent any recurrence.

6. Offsite incidents

Offsite incidents should be taken just as seriously as those on the company's own premises. The same procedures and actions as specified in Section 4 above should be implemented.

Environmental incident reporting
policy and procedure

If an environmental incident does occur, it needs to be reported to you immediately. And, in certain circumstances, you will need to report the incident to the relevant enforcement agency.

REPORTING AN ENVIRONMENTAL INCIDENT

You can't investigate an incident if you don't know about it. Your staff are used to reporting accidents when someone is injured, but reporting a spill or a leak isn't likely to get the same recognition. To help you find out what is happening, we've created an **Environmental Incident Reporting Policy and Procedure**. This will highlight to your staff the importance of reporting incidents that could cause harm to the environment. It gives details of actions to be taken directly after the incident and who might need to be informed.

ENVIRONMENTAL INCIDENT REPORTING
POLICY AND PROCEDURE

1. General statement

It is our policy that all identified environmental incidents will be given the utmost priority and employees are encouraged to promptly report all potential environmental incidents without delay.

As a company we operate a "no-blame" culture, as such no action will be taken against employees whose actions may have resulted in an environmental incident. The failure to report, or cover up a potential environmental incident is, however, viewed seriously.

The purpose of this Policy is to outline the procedures to be taken upon identifying a potential environmental incident. Therefore, all staff are expected to abide by the following procedures and co-operate with management in the event of an incident.

2. Action to be taken on discovering an incident

- if you suspect an incident has occurred, investigate at once but do not take risks

- if you discover an incident - stay calm

- raise the alarm by informing the nearest supervisor/site manager

- if it is safe to do so, try to control the incident by isolating plant/equipment and closing off any valves etc. Obtain help if necessary - but do not put yourself or others at risk

- direct all non-essential people away from the affected area

- activate the nearest fire alarm call point if an evacuation of the premises is required

- it may be possible to deal with small incidents/spills using the appropriate spill response kit and by closing doors/covering drains etc. to confine the emissions/discharges as far as possible

- follow specific instructions on the Material Safety Data Sheet. Confine and clean the spill with appropriate protective clothing and equipment

- for larger incidents, it may be necessary to inform the fire brigade, Environment Agency, local authority and/or water company, depending on its nature

- dispose of all waste and contaminated materials properly. If necessary, call the local Environmental Protection Team for information and assistance on disposal options.

3. Action to be taken following an incident

Every incident should be thoroughly investigated according to the company's Incident Investigation Policy and Procedure. Action should then be taken to ensure that the risk of a recurrence is minimised and that the relevant procedures have been reviewed and updated where necessary.

4. Further Information

The Environment Agency has prepared a simple generic "Pollution Incident Response Plan" (PPG21) which can be downloaded from their website http://publications. environment-agency.gov.uk/pdf/PMHO0204BHUP-e-e.pdf and completed for any site.

Environmental incident report

In the event of an environmental incident, it's wise to keep formal records of exactly what happened and what's been done about it.

INVESTIGATION PROCESS

If there's an environmental incident, all is not lost. If you can prove that you've identified, reported and acted on it, this will certainly help to mitigate potential enforcement action. To show to an inspector, or insurance assessor, and to help you keep a record of events, use our **Environmental Incident Report**. It's a simple to use document that helps you record basic facts and prioritise your actions.

Tip 1. Record as much information as you can - even things you don't think are that important. Make notes of who was called, what response you received, if an inspector intends to visit the site and anything else that you feel may help your case.

Tip 2. If you carry out any remedial works, or are given formal instructions from an enforcement officer, this information should definitely be recorded, again, in as much detail as possible.

Tip 3. Take photographs and attach them to your report. This sort of evidence can help you prove your innocence - especially if you can see that the source of the pollution is not on your site.

ENVIRONMENTAL INCIDENT REPORT

Company name:	**Incident ref no:**
Location of incident:	**Responsible person:**
Client contact details:	**Site manager details:**
Date and time of incident:	**Incident discovered by:**

Type of incident: Major Minor Near-miss	
Nature of incident:	
Environmental water pollution	Foul sewer pollution
Air pollution	Ecological damage
Land contamination	Spill
Waste (incorrect management)	Inappropriate storage
Architectural and heritage/conservation damage	Other damage, e.g. other property/company

Summary of incident:

Cause of incident:

Details of affected watercourse, groundwater, surface water drains or sewers:

What immediate corrective actions have been taken?:

Details of further action needed:

Incident reported to: Environment Agency Y/N Water company Y/N Local authority Y/N Other Y/N	**Third party contact details:**

Additional comments:

ENVIRONMENTAL INCIDENT REPORT GUIDANCE NOTES

Type of incident

Major. These include major damage to the ecosystem, major impact on property, or major damage to agriculture and/or commerce. Incidents such as these should be reported to the Environment Agency (EA).

Minor. These include, minor damage to the ecosystem, minor impact on property or minimal effect on quality. Incidents such as these needn't be reported to the EA.

Nature of incident

The following guidance should help you identify the type of environmental incident and what damage may have occurred.

Environmental water pollution. Has the incident affected a watercourse or groundwater by direct run-off or via a surface water drain?

Foul sewer pollution. Has the incident affected a water company or private foul sewage system? This is very important as it may damage a treatment plant or pumping station etc.

Air pollution. Has a toxic or obnoxious cloud affected the environment, or people and property?

Ecological damage. Has the incident done any obvious damage to the environment?

Land contamination. Has the incident done any damage to land on or off site? This may have serious cost implications.

Spill. Was the incident a result of a spillage of contaminating liquids or solids?

Waste (incorrect management). Was the incident a result of poor waste management practices?

Inappropriate storage. Was the incident a result of poor storage of polluting materials?

Architectural and heritage/conservation damage. Has the incident affected an important architectural or heritage site or a known conservation-designated site?

Details of affected watercourse/groundwater/surface water drains or sewers. If you are unsure of names etc., write what you know and describe positions for follow-up investigations.

Incident reported to. Inform the EA if thought to be major risk to groundwater or watercourse. It will inform drinking water abstractors if necessary.

Who to inform

- water company - if it's thought to impact foul sewer (mains drainage) or private treatment plant consent holder for others.
- local authority - if the incident poses an environmental health risk (odours/toxic clouds)
- neighbours, other landowners etc. - if they are at risk.

Reporting incidents to the Environment Agency

To report an environmental incident call the EA's **incident hotline** on **0800 80 70 60** (Freephone, 24 hour service). You should not use e-mail to report an incident, as this could delay the response.

Incidents the EA deals with:

- damage or danger to the natural environment
- pollution to water or land
- poaching or illegal fishing
- fish in distress or dead fish
- watercourse blocked by vehicle or fallen tree causing risk of flooding
- illegal dumping of hazardous waste or large amounts of industrial waste
- incidents at waste sites we regulate such as landfill, transfer station etc.
- illegal abstraction from watercourses
- unusual drop in riverflow
- collapsed or badly damaged river or canal banks.

Incidents the EA doesn't deal with:

- gas leaks
- burst water mains
- discolouration, odour or taste of drinking water
- flooding from domestic burst pipe or overflow from highway drains
- fly-tipping of household rubbish or small amounts of commercial waste
- domestic noise nuisance
- odours from domestic or small commercial premises

- burning domestic or garden waste

- domestic infestations

- smoke emissions from vehicles

- road maintenance

- interruptions to electricity or water supplies

- blocked domestic drains and sewers.

To report these issues, you should call your local authority or the appropriate utility company.

Environment incident - witness statement

Often staff or others will actually see an incident take place, so they may be able to give information which could prove vital. The best way of getting hold of this is through a formal interview.

What happened?

If there's a serious incident on your site, the first question you're likely to ask is: *"what happened?"* Often this information is relayed through colleagues in an informal manner and vital facts are lost. To help you find out exactly what occurred, why not use our **Witness Statement** document?

Formal interview

The first stage in this process is to conduct formal interviews with any witnesses.

Tip. Try to conduct these interviews before the end of the shift. This will ensure that facts aren't forgotten and, more importantly, not changed or embellished.

Why bother?

There's a common misconception that, following a serious incident, inspectors turn up with the single aim of taking enforcement action. Although this is one reason, they are also there to make sure that you're investigating the incident and taking steps to prevent another one. **Note.** An inspector may ask for staff interviews, which you are allowed to attend. If this happens, use our document to record what was said.

Make your intentions clear

When staff are asked questions in a formal manner they can often become defensive. This happens for a number of reasons. They may have a misguided sense of loyalty to their colleagues, or they might feel that their answers could get them into trouble.

Tip 1. Make it clear to whoever you're interviewing that your intentions are to find out what happened and to identify how you can prevent a further occurrence, not for gathering evidence to take disciplinary action etc.

Tip 2. You only want to know what they actually saw, not what they thought they saw, or even what a colleague told them they witnessed.

PUT IT ALL TOGETHER

Once you have completed all of the interviews, you should look for trends in the statements.

Tip. The most reliable pieces of information are likely to be those mentioned by more than one member of staff. But if one person states something completely different to their colleagues, re-interview them and ask them if they are sure about their response. Or simply discount it as unreliable.

ENVIRONMENT INCIDENT - WITNESS STATEMENT

WITNESS STATEMENT	
Name:	**Date and time of incident:** **Ref no:**
Work position:	**Telephone no:** **Mobile no:**
Address of witness:	
Location of incident:	
Names of others present and telephone nos:	
What were the likely consequences of this incident?	
Describe, to best of your knowledge, the incident details; include before, during, and after the incident.	
Did you take any photographs or video of the incident?	
Signature of witness: **Date and time of statement:**	This form is sheet 1 of .... *Please use continuation sheets if needed; on extra sheets just fill in Ref no and further descriptions as needed to link them.*

Non-conformance and corrective action record

Although we'd all like to think that we've done enough to manage potential environmental risks within our business, often this isn't the case. To help you to get back on track, you should formally record where you feel that improvements could be made and when they will be sorted.

CORRECTIVE ACTION

When undertaking environmental audits it's important to ensure that where environmental issues are not being managed or controlled as well as they could be, action is taken to resolve the problem and to prevent a recurrence. Our **Non-Conformance and Corrective Action Record** provides a tool to enable organisations to record such a situation and for managing the subsequent corrective and preventative action. Use this form to help you manage and track what action is being taken to overcome or resolve issues that may lead to an environmental incident.

Tip. This form can also be used following an environmental incident to record what remedial action was carried out.

NON-CONFORMANCE AND CORRECTIVE ACTION RECORD

Non-conformance identified through:	Audit ❏ Operations ❏	Emergency ❏ Operations ❏	Ref No.
Date:	Location:	Reported by:	

Description of Non-Conformance

Interim actions taken	Signature
	(Environmental Manager)

Additional planned actions	Target date	Date closed
Date completed:	Signature:	

Chapter 2

Environmental management systems

Construction - environmental management checklist

Environmental issues on construction sites should be managed properly, regardless of the size of the contract. Doing so can help to reduce waste and, in turn, your overheads. You can use our checklist to help you do this.

WHAT'S COVERED?

Our **Construction - Environmental Management Checklist** covers the main environmental issues that are likely to be found on a construction site. These include issues with Site Waste Management Plans, pollution prevention - notably from oil storage - waste management and recycling, and water use.

AUDIT

You can use our document to identify where you need to focus your efforts and to pinpoint where legal compliance issues may crop up. It can also be a valuable money-saving tool, helping you to identify what materials can be recycled or re-used instead of being sent to landfill. This saves on both waste handling fees and Landfill Tax.

CONSTRUCTION - ENVIRONMENTAL MANAGEMENT CHECKLIST

1.   *Project details*

Client:	
Site address:	
Contract start date:	
Contract duration:	
Date of inspection:	

2.   *Site Waste Management Plan*

	Yes	No	Comments
Do the Site Waste Management Plan (SWMP) Regulations apply to this site?			**Note.** Different SWMPs apply to projects costing between £300,000 and £500,000 or those from £500,000 upwards.
If yes, has a plan been introduced?			
Is the SWMP held on site?			
Is the plan up-to-date?			
Does the plan contain supporting documentation such as waste transfer notes, etc.?			

3.   *Raw materials - inspection, storage and use*

	Yes	No	Comments
Are there adequate storage facilities for raw materials on site?			
Are materials inspected on arrival?			

	Yes	No	Comments
Are stock levels maintained to suit the work as the project develops?			
Is there any evidence of over ordering?			
Is there any evidence of damage to stored materials?			
Can good quality off-cuts etc. of raw materials be re-used?			

4. Materials management

	Yes	No	Comments
Can breakage and damage to materials be reduced through better materials management?			
Does spillage occur when materials are transferred?			
Are staff trained to deal with spillages, e.g. in the use of spill kits etc.?			
If fuels, chemicals and paints etc. are stored on site, are they adequately bunded to control leakage?			
Are quantities of oil held on site, in excess of 200 litres? If so, are suitable bunds (that hold 110% of the storage capacity of the oil tank) in place?			
Is oil storage away from watercourses and drainage?			
Are there any problems on site with oils or chemicals leaking into watercourses?			

5.   *Packaging*

	Yes	No	Comments
Are there designated disposal routes for transit packaging (e.g. pallets, slip-sheets, shrink wrap)?			
Are raw material containers re-used for transporting materials within the process?			
Is raw material packaging recycled?			
Are there any ways of minimising packaging by agreement with suppliers and customers?			
Can any packaging for products be re-used in the workplace or elsewhere?			
Is any packaging returned to suppliers for re-use?			
Is any waste electrical and electronic equipment (WEEE) generated on site?			
Is the process for disposing of WEEE understood?			

6.   *Water usage*

	Yes	No	Comments
Has all surface water and foul drainage on site been identified?			
Is there evidence of run-off from spoil heaps?			
Is there evidence of vehicle/machinery washing, and, if so, is run-off contained?			
Are all hosepipes fitted with triggers?			
Is water usage being monitored?			

7.   *Waste*

	Yes	No	Comments
Have defined areas been set aside for waste storage?			
Are all waste receptacles suitably marked?			
Are skip sizes appropriate and emptied regularly?			
Are inactive waste streams segregated to ensure that the correct landfill tax tariff is applied?			
Is it possible to rationalise the number of waste collections?			
Did you shop around local waste contractors to find the best option for your business?			
Are materials collected separately for recycling?			
Are recyclables visible in the general skip?			
Are pallets re-used/recycled?			
Are any hazardous wastes generated on site?			
Is waste documentation held on site?			
Are copies of carrier licences held?			
Is the site manager aware of duty-of-care?			
Is there any evidence of fly-tipping or waste dumped on site by non-construction site personnel?			

Checklist completed by: .... *(Print name)*

Signed:................................   Date ....

Contractor appraisal questionnaire - environment

Before you appoint contractors to undertake construction work, it's a good idea to check out their environmental credentials. You can do this by adding some supplementary environmental questions to your Contractor Appraisal Questionnaire.

GREEN EVALUATION

Our **Contractor Appraisal Questionnaire** covers the kind of checks you need to make before appointing construction contractors and is based on health and safety law. But if you want to check the contractor's environmental performance, you can do so by sending out this supplementary questionnaire.

The questions cover a range of issues including policy, responsibilities, competent advice, emergency procedures, monitoring, training, statutory registrations and past enforcement action.

CONTRACTOR APPRAISAL QUESTIONNAIRE - ENVIRONMENT

1. Do you have an environmental policy statement?

Yes ❑ No ❑

If "Yes", please provide a copy.

2. Who has overall responsibility for environmental matters within your organisation?

Name:	Position:

3. Who is appointed to provide competent advice on environmental matters?

Name:	Contact details:
Position:	Qualifications: (attach separate details if preferred)

4. Has the company carried out an environmental impact assessment and set environmental objectives as a result?

Yes ❑ No ❑

If "Yes", please provide details.

5. Has your environmental management system been externally assessed, e.g. as part of a competency assessment scheme, ISO14001 etc.?

Yes ❑ No ❑

If "Yes", please provide details and, where applicable, a copy of the certificate.

6. Does your company carry any legally required environmental registrations as a result of your work activities?

Yes ❑ No ❑

If "Yes", please provide details of the registrations you hold and copies of certificates, e.g. licensed waste carrier, packaging recovery scheme registration, hazardous waste producer registration.

7. Attach details of any environmental enforcement notices received or prosecutions over the past two years. Use a separate sheet if required.

8. Do you have procedures for dealing with environmental incidents, such as spillages?

Yes ❑   No ❑

If "Yes", please attach details.

9. Do you have arrangements for minimising waste, recycling and segregating waste in accordance with your duty of care?

Yes ❑   No ❑

If "Yes", please attach details.

10. Please describe your arrangements for environmental monitoring of site work.

11. Please describe your arrangements for training staff in your environmental policy and procedures, including emergency arrangements.

12. Questionnaire completed by:

Name:

Company/position:

Telephone :

E-mail:

Date:

Environmental policy statement

Making a public statement on your commitment to the environment is becoming increasingly popular. Although it's not a legal requirement, many businesses will ask to see your policy regarding how you deal with environmental issues. And indicators suggest that these requests will increase.

ENVIRONMENTAL COMMITMENT

How are you going to manage your environmental issues? Are they going to be formally addressed? This is the type of question our **Environmental Policy Statement** raises. Unlike a health and safety policy statement, there isn't a legal requirement to complete one, and there's no restriction on what you say in it. Our sample policy can be taken as it is or modified to suit your business, or you can just use it as guidance to create your own. The policy is simply a way for you to show your intentions and provide a base from which you can develop whatever management controls are necessary to stay on the right side of the law and reduce your potential impacts, wherever practicable. Once completed, we'd advise you publicise the fact to your staff in a prominent place, such as a notice board, so that they're fully aware of the commitment you've made.

ENVIRONMENTAL POLICY STATEMENT

.... *(insert company name)*

.... *(insert company name)* is a professional and environmentally conscious organisation, which acknowledges the impact that our operations may potentially have on the environment. The clear objective of .... *(insert company name)* is to minimise any impact on the environment by:

- preventing pollution, reducing waste and ensuring, wherever practicable, that measures are implemented to protect and preserve natural habitats, flora and fauna

- considering the effects that our operations may have on the local community

- taking action to eliminate or reduce, as far as practicable, any potentially adverse environmental impacts

- promoting environmental awareness amongst our suppliers, contractors and partners by implementation of operational procedures

- seeking to work in partnership with the community by behaving in a considerate and socially responsible manner

- ensuring effective and expedient incident control, investigation and reporting.

Managerial and supervisory staff have responsibilities for the implementation of the policy and must ensure that environmental issues are given adequate consideration in the planning and day-to-day supervision of all work.

.... *(insert company name)* will fully comply with the duties placed upon it within the requirements of legislation, whilst at all times complying with, as a matter of best practice, the requirements and duties set out within Approved Guidance as issued by the Environment Agency and other organisations. As part of the company's commitment to maintaining the highest levels of environmental management, it is the intention that the company will work towards environmental management systems compliant with ISO14001.

All employees and sub-contractors are expected to co-operate and assist in the implementation of this policy, whilst ensuring that their own works, so far as is reasonably practicable, are carried out without risk to themselves, others or the environment. This includes co-operating with management on any environment related matter.

. . . . *(insert company name)* will take all practical steps to ensure that potential hazards and risks to the environment are identified and that suitable and effective preventive and control measures are implemented. All employees will be provided with the necessary resources, equipment, information, instruction and training to fulfill the requirements of this policy.

The directors have overall responsibility for all environmental matters. The operation of this policy and the associated procedures will be monitored and reviewed on a regular basis to ensure that they remain current and applicable to the company's activities. This policy has been endorsed by the board of directors which gives its full support to its implementation.

Signed: . . . .   Date: . . . .

Managing Director (or equivalent)

Environmental management
organisational structure

To ensure that environmental issues are dealt with it's vital that your staff know what their responsibilities are and who they should report any problems to. The simplest way of doing this is to create a clear structure.

WHO DOES WHAT?

Ignoring environmental management issues could cost you dearly, not only through lost time and enforcement action, but also in clean-up costs. So to manage the issues properly all staff need to be completely clear about what they should be doing and to whom they should report. To ensure that everyone is clear, use our **Environmental Management Organisational Structure** document.

HOW TO USE OUR DOCUMENT

The first part is an organisation chart. This should be amended to suit your own business. Names of directors, managers and even selected employees (any who have specific duties with regards to environmental management) should be added.

Tip. Anyone who features on the management chart should be given a copy of the whole document. They should then formally agree any duties that they have been assigned.

ENVIRONMENTAL MANAGEMENT
ORGANISATIONAL STRUCTURE

The following organisation chart outlines the structure for the management of environmental issues within the company.

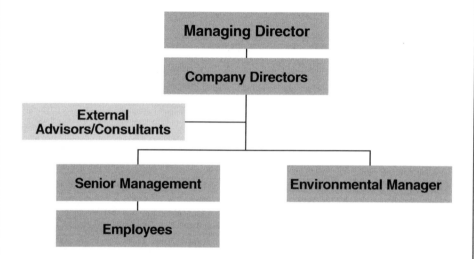

The effectiveness of the management of environmental issues is dependent on the action of those responsible for ensuring that all aspects of work are carried out with due consideration for the environment.

Ultimate responsibility lies with the directors, but specific duties are delegated to others according to their experience and training.

Company directors and senior management, both individually and collectively, will ensure that this policy is applied throughout the company and that those employed by the company are kept fully informed of its content.

Managers will ensure that this policy is adopted by all employees, sub-contractors, suppliers and visitors. Furthermore, every individual person will be informed of the specific duty of care that they have in relation to environmental management.

IMPLEMENTATION

Whilst overall responsibility for the implementation of this organisational structure is vested with the company directors, responsibility for the day-to-day application of the policy is delegated to the director responsible for environmental management.

To clarify the roles and responsibilities, the following duties have been allocated to nominated employees:

Induction training . . . . *(insert name)*

Environmental impact/risk assessments . . . . *(insert name)*

Workplace environmental audits . . . . *(insert name)*

Waste management . . . . *(insert name)*

Noise assessments and control . . . . *(insert name)*

Air emissions (smoke, fumes, dust, etc.) . . . . *(insert name)*

Fuel, oil and chemical storage . . . . *(insert name)*

These individuals will be responsible for ensuring that adequate consideration is given to each of the various issues. However, in some instances, specialist advice and support may be required to enable them to ensure that a suitable and sufficient assessment of the issues has been undertaken.

All individuals are, however, expected to:

- take reasonable care for the protection of the environment through their own acts or omissions

- co-operate with others in the discharge of their duties

- work in accordance with all environmental procedures.

When planning work activities, full account is to be taken of those factors that help to eliminate potentially harmful emissions/discharges, waste or other forms of pollution such as noise. Decisions about other priorities (e.g. programme and profit) are to take proper account of the environmental constraints that may be present.

Specific and precise arrangements should be developed and implemented, as needed, to enable the company's Environmental Management Policy to be properly implemented. Safe systems of work, incorporating, where applicable, environmental reviews and risk assessments, are to be established, implemented and monitored to ensure the appropriate environmental standards are being maintained at all times.

High standards will be applied when complying with legislation regarding the protection of the environment.

All incidents, no matter how minor, will be reported and recorded on an Environmental Incident Report form. Significant incidents will be promptly investigated to ensure that the appropriate preventive measures are implemented to prevent a recurrence.

All such incidents should be reported to the company's nominated Environmental Manager.

Environmental training programmes will be promoted with the object of achieving personal awareness of the risks and hazards to the environment associated with the works we undertake.

Responsibility and accountability in relation to the prevention of pollution, reduction of waste and protection of the environment will be specified clearly and in writing to all employees.

Arrangements for the implementation of this structure are the responsibility of the company's directors.

This Policy will be explained to all new staff as part of their induction training and a copy of the Policy will be made available for reference by any member of staff.

An annual review of this Policy will be carried out to ensure that the procedures and control measures remain valid and relevant to our work activities. Further reviews may be carried out as and when required. All updates and amendments to the documentation will be circulated to all company personnel.

Environmental management responsibilities

Making roles and responsibilities crystal clear to directors, managers and staff will help to minimise the risks of an environmental incident taking place. It will also help to ensure the success of any "green" schemes.

MANAGEMENT RESPONSIBILITIES

Rather than just hoping that staff will follow your environmental policy, having defined responsibilities will help ensure your policy is adhered to. To assist you in deciding what these duties should actually be, use our **Environmental Management Responsibilities** document.

Tip. This document should be amended to suit the particular needs of your organisation. If you feel that some individuals should have additional, or fewer, duties then you should amend it accordingly. However, overall responsibility should always remain with the managing director of your company.

Note. This document should be used in conjunction with our **Environmental Management Organisational Structure** document.

ENVIRONMENTAL MANAGEMENT RESPONSIBILITIES

Managing Director

The Managing Director has overall responsibility for the Environmental Policy and its implementation.

Company Directors

All directors will ensure that:

- the Environmental Policy is issued to all employees

- all employees are made aware of their personal responsibilities

- appropriate training, resources and support are to be made available to all staff

- environmental issues are to be given appropriate consideration

- they regularly liaise with the Environmental Manager

- risks to the Company relating to potential incidents at work, environmental impacts, loss or damage to Company property, and risks to the public through the Company's activities are properly evaluated

- liability is covered by appropriate insurance and that advice is given to the extent to which risks are acceptable, whether insured or not

- environmental performance is recorded and reviewed periodically so as to advise when action is necessary to correct adverse trends.

It is the responsibility of the directors to ensure the allocation of adequate finances and other resources for the effective implementation of the Environmental Management system. Key topics requiring specific resource allocation are: Management representation; Training; Emergency response equipment; Monitoring and measuring equipment, and Record-keeping systems.

Environmental Manager

The Environmental Manager is responsible for overseeing the management of environmental issues within the company, as follows:

- report to the directors and keep them appraised on all matters regarding environmental management

- state the Company's policies in writing with regard to environmental management and ensure it is brought to the attention of all employees

- ensure that arrangements are made for implementing the Company's Environmental Policy

- ensure that environmental management data is collected, reviewed and reported on

- ensure that Company procedures, instructions and guidance are regularly reviewed and amended as necessary

- provide environmental advice to managers, employees and customers using, as necessary, specialist external advisors/consultants

- promote positive environmental values throughout the Company

- communicate effectively with external organisations, such as the Environment Agency, regarding the policy and its implementation

- investigate environmental incidents and record all findings and make recommendations for the prevention of similar incidents

- liaise with procurement and project managers on contract standards and any future changes or additions required to the policy

- monitor the effectiveness of the procedures by workplace inspections and audits and report on any improvements that may be required.

Senior Management

Directors and managers are, at all times, responsible for implementation of the Company's Environmental Policy. All members of the senior management team shall:

- understand the Company's Environmental Policy

- set a positive personal example

- identify and organise appropriate training for their staff

- liaise with the company's Environmental Manager

- actively promote a positive environmental culture throughout their areas of responsibility

- ensure the Policy is implemented properly and that any delegated duties are correctly performed

- ensure that all agreed actions are implemented as soon as practicable

- suspend any work or other activity which is considered to constitute an immediate danger to the environment. The circumstances should then be fully investigated and no work shall be allowed to continue until the appropriate remedial action has been taken.

- ensure that regular environmental inspections are carried out and that environmental issues are actively managed and controlled

- ensure that the overall environmental performance of company sites is discussed at regular intervals with all contractors and sub-contractors

- report any problems or improvements to this Policy to the appropriate director

- actively promote, at all levels, the Company's commitment to effective environmental management.

All employees

All employees are required to:

- understand the Company's Environmental Policy

- co-operate with the Company in complying with duties and requirements imposed by relevant statutory provisions and Company procedures

- co-operate with the Company in complying with environmental management duties and requirements imposed by management

- not interfere with, or misuse anything provided in the interests of environmental protection

- report all environmental incidents to your manager.

Environmental audit checklist

Completing a formal audit of how your business might have an environmental impact - either positive or negative - is a good starting point for prioritising actions and developing plans.

ENVIRONMENTAL AUDIT CHECKLIST AND GUIDANCE NOTE

Do you know what impact your business is having on the environment? Have you ever checked? If not, an audit is a good place to start. Our **Environmental Audit Checklist** and its guidance document will help you identify any key impacts, possible breaches of legislation (you might not even know about) and control measures which will help you either reduce the impact or achieve legal compliance. This audit process should also save you money by reducing energy costs, preventing spills and by helping to ward off enforcement action. Use this checklist as a starting point and a tool with which to check your progress.

ENVIRONMENTAL AUDIT CHECKLIST

Site address:	Project/Ref No:
Client:	Date:

Item	Satisfactory			Action required to rectify deficiencies	Priority
	Y	N	N/A		
Site security					
Complaints					
Waste management					
Cleaning operations					
Hazardous & special wastes					
Chemicals & fuels					
Water pollution prevention					
Pollution response					
Dust & air pollution					
Light pollution					
Noise & vibration					
Visual impact					
Permits, licences & consents					
Nature conservation & countryside protection					
Heritage & archaeology					

The following guidance is designed to highlight some of the environmental aspects that should be considered when completing the Environment Audit Checklist.

Item	Points to consider
Site security	Integrity of perimeter fencing, gates, lighting and signage. Ensure that the keys are removed from all plant, liaise with police/council, check alarm systems and ensure that security arrangements are in place.
Complaints	Check with the site manager and client to determine if any environmental complaints have been received from local residents or other interested parties.
Waste management	Ensure all wastes are properly stored in segregated skips and check to see if storage containers are leaking or overflowing. Skips and other receptacles should be covered to prevent any accumulation of rainwater and to help prevent waste from being blown away. Ensure waste is being properly disposed of and that copies of the Waste Transfer Notes are available.
Cleaning operations	Where cleaning activities could result in contaminated effluent or chemicals draining into any foul or surface water sewer, ensure that appropriate arrangements are in place to prevent any such contamination and that the area is properly bunded and drains are clear of debris.
Hazardous & special waste	These include waste oils, solvents, acids, wood preservatives and batteries. Ensure hazardous wastes are properly stored, ensure that all hazardous waste is disposed of by authorised persons/authorities, Check Waste Transfer Notes in place.
Chemicals & fuels	Ensure all such substances are stored within bunded areas, the bund should contain 110% of the maximum volume of the container/tank. Drip trays should be used to catch any drips or leaks from portable equipment and spill kits must be provided near storage and refuelling points. Check for leaks or damage to bunds and containers and ensure the storage facilities are secure and safe from vandalism.
Prevention of water pollution	All deliveries should be supervised with bunding provided around all storage areas; spill kits should be readily available, concrete wash-out areas should be carefully positioned to prevent pollution of watercourses, drains or the subsoil/groundwater.

Item	Points to consider
Pollution response	Appropriate spill kits are to be provided at key locations around the site, this should include all refuelling and storage areas. Emergency spill procedures and contact numbers are to be prominently displayed and communicated to all staff on site.
Dust & air pollution	All operations likely to cause excessive dust, such as the cutting of concrete, use of road saws, excavations of loose dry material and vehicle movements during dry weather should be carefully controlled and the use of water sprays, wheel washes and sheeted stockpiles shall be considered. Road sweepers to keep roads clean and the maintenance of plant and equipment shall also be adopted to minimise emissions of dust and exhaust fumes etc.
Light pollution	Ensure that any temporary site lighting does not cause a nuisance to neighbours, give careful consideration of the position of such lighting and where appropriate erect barriers and screens in mitigation.
Noise & vibration	Ensure any noise reduction measures and barriers are in place and operational. Plant should be well maintained and regularly inspected with the most suitable plant for the job being used, this will help to prevent both noise and vibration issues. Ensure that all plant is turned off when not in use to help reduce and eliminate any unnecessary noise pollution.
Visual impact	Regular checks should be made to ensure that the site is clean and tidy in appearance. The approach to the site should be clear of obstructions and no employee or contractor vehicles should be allowed to park on the approach roads.
Permits, licences & consents	All permits, consents and necessary licences are in place and valid for the relevant works.
Nature conservation & countryside protection	Consider the impact that any works may potentially have on local flora and fauna.
Heritage & archaeology	Has the local authority archaeological service been informed of any significant historical features or discoveries on or near the site of the works.

Environmental benchmarking and

performance indicators

Gauging the success or failure of a scheme is very difficult without evidence that is clear and concise. The best way to achieve this is to create meaningful benchmarks and use industry standard calculations.

IDENTIFY YOUR ENVIRONMENTAL PERFORMANCE

The establishment of meaningful environmental benchmarks is often a difficult and emotive subject. However, a growing interest in the development and recording of such environmental performance indicators is now being seen. So if you're asked to provide this information or if you simply want to identify your own environmental performance, use our **Environmental Benchmarking and Performance Indicators** table. Once you have the information required, you'll then be able to set goals and target areas in which minor or even more significant improvements can be made.

ENVIRONMENTAL BENCHMARKING AND PERFORMANCE INDICATORS

The basic aim of a performance indicator is to enable a company to assess its own performance and benchmark itself against established standards and the performance achieved by other companies.

Typical environmental performance indicators

The following table outlines a number of simple to use and easy to measure environmental performance indicators which can be used by almost all types of organisation.

Indicator	Measurement units	Comments
Water use	M3/product output	Water is a vital resource and in some parts of the country is increasingly scarce. Implement water efficiency measures to reduce the level of water use.
Recycling and reuse of water	%	Water recycling and reuse can save natural resources and reduce production costs.
Use of renewable and alternative fuels	%	The use of alternative and renewable fuel does not contribute to the depletion of fossil resources and causes lower air emissions than the use of conventional fuels.
Total waste	Kg/product output	Waste disposal can cause air, water and soil pollution. There is also a significant cost associated with the disposal of waste.
Non-hazardous waste disposed	Kg/product output	
Hazardous waste disposed	Kg/product output	
Recycled waste	Kg/product output	Recycling reduces the need for waste disposal.
Recycling rate	%	
Nuisance complaints	number/1,000 units product output	Complaints are an indicator of environmental impact, for example noise and odour.
Upheld cases of prosecution	number/1,000 units product output	Prosecution suggests a serious breach of environmental legislation and is a key performance indicator for the quality of the environmental management.

Notes:

Units can be changed to suit different businesses, such as "Number/100 man hours" or "Kg/Employee".

Indicators can be compared with other local/national companies and with previous year's figures, where available.

Target figures should be established and worked towards each year, progressively tighter, but realistic targets should be aimed for each year.

Environmental purchasing policy

Using our Environmental Purchasing Policy will help you to fulfil your environmental responsibilities and influence your suppliers, so that you can justifiably claim that you are "greening the supply chain".

WHAT'S COVERED?

All companies have purchasing procedures, which may be under the control of a purchasing department or, on a smaller scale, the responsibility of a particular member of staff. Either way, you should ensure that everyone involved in your purchasing procedure is made aware of this policy and acts upon it accordingly. Its aim is to encourage the purchase of goods and services which are environmentally-acceptable, perform well and achieve best value for money overall.

KEEP IT UP-TO-DATE

It should be a "live" document, meaning you regularly review your purchasing procedures and audit it to ensure that it meets with your commitments. Therefore, we've provided space to insert a review date, e.g. in twelve months. There's also a space for the policy statement to be signed and dated. This should be completed by whoever is responsible for environmental management within your business.

ENVIRONMENTAL PURCHASING POLICY

……………………………….. *(insert name of company)*

……………………………….. *(insert name of company)* recognises the critical need to ensure its sustainability by carrying out its purchasing activities in an environmentally responsible manner.

We will give preference to purchasing environmentally preferable products and services that meet current performance, safety and regulatory requirements. Our Company will continue to source and increase the purchase of products and services that are deemed "environmentally preferable".

We shall therefore undertake to develop purchasing by having regard to quality and cost, which includes:

- specifying wherever possible and reasonably practicable, the use of environmentally friendly or sustainable materials and products

- promoting the use of long lasting and recyclable products

- not using environmentally damaging products where an alternative (product or method) is available

- investigating if it is necessary to purchase the product

- sourcing and purchasing items from local producers and suppliers, wherever possible

- ensuring that all specifications contain a facility for potential suppliers to submit prices for environmentally friendly alternatives.

All purchasing will promote the use of the least environmentally damaging products, i.e. to place a preference, where design and safety factors allow, on goods which are:

- durable, reusable, refillable or recyclable

- recycled or contain reused materials

- from a proven sustainable source

- energy efficient

- designed to cause minimal damage to the environment in their production, distribution, use and disposal

- economically viable and meet the requirements of value for money and quality.

This Environmental Purchasing Policy will be an ongoing procedure to be reviewed at least annually and will take into account both changing circumstances and improved environmental awareness within the Company.

Signed ....

Date..

This Policy will be reviewed on .... *(insert date)*

Guidance note - types of environmental management system

If you're considering formalising the way you manage environmental issues by implementing one of the many formal management systems, which one should you go for? It's a choice that should not be made lightly, as picking the wrong one could cost you dearly.

WHICH SYSTEM?

We've created a **Guidance Note - Types of Environmental Management System**, that provides further information on formally accredited systems. The guidance also includes further information on the different types of management system, such as ISO and EMAS, and the standards against which they're monitored. This information can then be used to assist in determining what type is best for your organisation or if, indeed, you need one at all.

GUIDANCE NOTE - TYPES OF ENVIRONMENTAL MANAGEMENT SYSTEM

An environmental management system (EMS) provides a framework for managing environmental responsibilities so that they become more efficient and more integrated into overall operations. An EMS should form an integral element of a company's corporate management system. An EMS allows a company to understand, describe and control its significant impacts on the environment, reduce the risk of potentially costly pollution incidents, ensure compliance with environmental legislation and continually improve its business operations.

There are three formal environmental management systems/schemes:

- **ISO 14001** Environmental Management System standard

- **EMAS** - EU Eco-Management and Audit Scheme

- **BS8555** - Environmental Management Systems - Guide to phased implementation of an EMS including the use of environmental performance evaluation.

An EMS should ensure that the company's activities are in accordance with the environmental policy. For any company wanting to improve its environmental performance, establishing an environmental policy is a good place to start.

What is ISO 14001?

ISO 14001 is applicable to all types and sizes of organisation and is an international voluntary standard. It does not state specific environmental performance criteria but describes the core requirements for environmental management necessary for certification.

The principle behind ISO 14001 is continual improvement in environmental performance. The basic approach is:

- establishment of environmental policy

- planning: legal requirements, objective and target setting, establishing a management programme

- implementation and operation: responsibilities, training, document and operational control

- checking and corrective action: monitoring and measurement, non-conformance and corrective action, procedures and EMS auditing; and

- management review: assess progress against defined policy, objectives and procedures.

Third party certification to ISO 14001 is by an accredited certification body, although organisations can elect to make a self-declaration of compliance.

What is EMAS?

The Eco-Management and Audit Scheme (EMAS), is a voluntary EU-wide initiative which requires organisations to produce a public statement about their environmental performance and have that statement independently verified. The organisation is then recognised and rewarded for going beyond the minimum legal compliance and continuously improving their environmental performance.

EMAS requires participating organisations to implement an EMS which must meet the requirements of the international standard ISO 14001. So EMAS is a natural progression from ISO 14001 with organisations maintaining registration to both.

What is BS8555?

Building on ISO 14001 and EMAS, BS8555 provides guidance to companies on the phased implementation, maintenance and improvement of a formal EMS.

BS8555 makes particular reference to small and medium sized enterprises (SMEs) but is applicable to companies of any size, regardless of the type of work or location of the business. It outlines an implementation process that can be undertaken in six separate phases and allows for phased acknowledgement of progress towards the full implementation of an accredited EMS, such as ISO 14001. The advantage of adopting the BS 8555 methodology is that an ISO 14001 compliant system can be progressively developed and implemented within the workplace in a controlled and structured manner that is more likely to be suited to SMEs with limited resources.

Chapter 3

Statutory nuisance

Guidance note - how to avoid creating

a statutory nuisance

A statutory nuisance can be attributed to the poor state of your premises or any noise, odour, smoke, fumes, gas, dust steam, noxious vapours, the keeping of animals, deposits and accumulations of refuse or other substances escaping from your premises.

LEGAL POSITION

Unfortunately, no legal definition of a statutory nuisance exists. However, for action to be taken, the nuisance complained of must be, or is likely to be, harmful to a person's health, or interfere with their legitimate use and enjoyment of their property/land.

Note. Part III of the **Environmental Protection Act 1990** contains the main legislation relating to statutory nuisance. It applies in England, Wales and Scotland and is enforced by local authorities.

GENERAL GUIDANCE NOTE ON STATUTORY NUISANCE

To help you identify and understand the legal aspects of creating a statutory nuisance we've produced a **Guidance Note - How to Avoid Creating a Statutory Nuisance**. It includes basic guidance on the everyday actions that can be taken to reduce the likelihood of creating a statutory nuisance and gives details on what can happen if you fail to manage one properly.

GUIDANCE NOTE - HOW TO AVOID CREATING A STATUTORY NUISANCE

In most cases it is relatively easy to prevent the occurrence of a statutory nuisance, or to resolve potential issues. The following points provide basic guidance on the everyday actions that can be taken to reduce the likelihood of creating a statutory nuisance:

- establish what could constitute a potential nuisance to neighbours by checking noise, odours, dust, fumes, waste and other emissions that may be generated by your business, near to the boundary of your site. Be sure to review the situation during different operating conditions and at different times of the day and consider what changes/measures could be introduced to prevent or minimise potential nuisances

- maintain a positive relationship with your neighbours, particularly in relation to temporary effects that are likely to impact on them

- always inform neighbours in advance if you believe that a particular operation, such as building work or the installation of new plant or equipment, could cause an adverse effect. Neighbours are less likely to complain if kept informed, as they will perceive the business as more considerate and understanding

- even if minor issues are raised which do not amount to a statutory nuisance, it is always worth considering what can be done to improve the situation

- ensure all staff are aware of the need to avoid nuisances. Regularly check your site for any waste, accumulations, evidence of vermin, noise or odours as applicable

- where practicable, schedule or restrict noisy activities to the normal working day and consider how noisy operations may impact on those close to the site boundaries. Where practicable, consider relocating noisy operations further away from site boundaries, or make use of existing features as noise barriers

- minimise general noise pollution from your buildings by, for example, keeping doors and windows closed

- reduce noise levels by increasing insulation to the building fabric and keeping doors and windows closed

- ensure that any intruder and fire alarm systems on your premises have a maintenance contract and a callout agreement to reduce the occurrence of malfunctions and false alarms

- consider replacing any noisy equipment and take account of noise emissions when buying new or replacement equipment

- don't burn any waste materials on site.

How do I know if a nuisance exists?

If you are responsible for having caused a statutory nuisance, it is likely that your local Environmental Health Officer would have received complaints. However, a complaint does not in itself confirm that a nuisance exists.

If your Environmental Health Officer assesses that a statutory nuisance exists or is likely to occur, the local authority is duty bound to serve an abatement notice. Such a notice can:

- require you to abate the nuisance, i.e. to lessen or reduce it

- prohibit or restrict the nuisance

- require you to carry out works or other steps to abate, restrict or remove the nuisance.

Enforcement may not always come through statutory bodies such as the local Environmental Health Officer, as individuals can also take legal action against you and/or your business under the same legislation.

Always discuss statutory nuisance issues with your Environmental Health Officer and remember that an abatement notice is a legal notice and non-compliance with it could result in a prosecution being taken out against you and/or your company. If you believe an abatement notice has been incorrectly or improperly served, you can appeal against it.

Statutory nuisance

Organisations have a duty to ensure that their actions and operations do not unreasonably impact on their neighbours or on the enjoyment of their property. Consideration therefore needs to be given to be management and elimination of potential nuisances. A failure to do so could result in any of the following:

- negative publicity in the local/national press

- loss of contracts due to perceived lack of concern over environmental issues

- enforcement action being taken by the local Environmental Health Officer

- private action being taken by local residents.

All of these consequences could impact on the operation and profitability of your organisation.

Dust management checklist

Failure to manage dust properly is likely to provoke complaints from neighbours. If there is dust on your site that could cause a problem, you should work out where it could be blown to, and identify how you intend to control it. Keep records of your survey and plans.

DUST MANAGEMENT

If you have clouds of dust blowing into gardens or covering cars, you're not going to be too popular with your neighbours and are likely to get a complaint. To help reduce the chances of this happening we've produced a **Dust Management Checklist**, which can be used to conduct a formal assessment of your site. Use the document to identify any possible sources of dust, likely areas in which it may build up and, most importantly, what you're going to do to prevent it becoming a nuisance. The second part gives some handy tips and guidance on what steps you can take to minimise dust problems.

DUST MANAGEMENT CHECKLIST

Company name:	Ref. no:
Site location/address:	Site manager/responsible person:
	Site manager contact details:

Type of assessment:	❏ Routine	❏ Reactive	❏ Other

Environmental conditions

Prevailing wind direction:	❏ North ❏ East ❏ South ❏ West ❏ NE ❏ NW ❏ SE ❏ SW
Average wind speed:	. . . . mph
Maximum wind speed:	. . . . mph
Ambient temperature:	. . . . °C
Weather conditions:	❏ Dry ❏ Wet ❏ Raining ❏ Overcast ❏ Sunny

Site description:

Origin/source of dust generation:
(i.e. stack emissions, manufacturing processes, excavations, road dust etc.)

Type of dust:
(i.e. sawdust, soil, construction dust etc.)

Details of control measures:
(i.e. use of water suppression sprays, exclusion zones, road sweepers etc.)

Details of any further action needed:

Additional comments:

Tips for avoiding dust problems on site:

The checklist below can be used to help minimise dust problems:

- locate stockpiles of loss materials out of the wind (or cover them) to minimise the potential for dust generation

- keep stockpiles to the minimum height and use gentle slopes

- minimise the storage time of materials on site

- store materials away from site boundaries and downwind of sensitive areas

- ensure that all dust-generating materials are transported to and from site are covered by a tarpaulin

- minimise the height of fall of materials

- avoid spillage and clean up as soon as possible

- damp down areas with potential to generate dust clouds

- minimise abrasive cutting and grinding operations which may cause excessive dust on site

- use dust extractors on cutters and saws or a wet cutting technique

- spray water during cutting of paving slabs and concrete to minimise dust generation

- clean the wheels of vehicles leaving the site so that mud is not spread on surrounding roads - dry mud turns to dust

- use enclosed chutes for dropping rubble to ground level - the disposal of demolition materials have the potential to cause dust, debris and damage to the ground

- locate crushing plant away from sensitive sites - consider siting within buildings where possible.

Waste management checklist

If waste isn't controlled properly, you could end up with a vermin problem. You may also get complaints from neighbours because of smells or because items have blown on to their property.

WASTE MANAGEMENT

Waste isn't just an issue when it leaves your site, it can also cause you problems before it has been taken away. Waste can be a statutory nuisance simply if large amounts of it are visible, it creates a nasty smell or it encourages vermin. So you'll need to make sure it's managed properly. To help, we've produced a **Waste Management Checklist**, which will assist you in managing your waste so it won't create a nuisance to your neighbours.

WASTE MANAGEMENT CHECKLIST

Company name:	Ref. no:		
Site location/address:	Site manager/responsible person:		
	Site manager contact details:		
Type of assessment:	❏ Routine	❏ Reactive	❏ Other

Description/type of waste: *(i.e. liquid, solid, granular, commercial, industrial, hazardous, non-hazardous,* *domestic, etc.)*
Origin/source of waste: *(i.e. fly tipped material, excess material from works on site, by-product, waste from* *site, unknown source, etc.)*
Nuisances associated with the waste: *(i.e. visual, odours, vermin infestation, insect infestation, obstruction, etc.)*
Duration/timing: *(i.e. when was the waste deposited, how long has it been there, etc.)*
Details of control measures: *(i.e. is the waste covered, contained in skips, within a specific waste area, located away* *from neighbours, etc.)*
Details of any further action needed:
Additional comments:

Tips for avoiding waste problems on site:

The checklist below can be used to help minimise waste problems on site:

- carry out a walk-through survey to identify potential sources of waste and refuse

- ensure skips, bins and other waste containers are covered and are in a good state of repair

- ensure that waste material is regularly collected and removed from site

- do not allow waste to accumulate unnecessarily

- check for signs of vermin (rats/mice) and if necessary look to eradicate the problem through a combination of waste removal/disposal and pest control

- check for signs of insects and fly infestations which could spread disease

- ensure that putrescible wastes are not left outside to decay and decompose

- ensure that waste containing food or food matter is properly disposed of and does not cause an attraction for vermin, dogs/cats or other animals

- ensure that all hazardous wastes are properly controlled and disposed of in accordance with the appropriate disposal routes

- ensure that litter and other waste is not allowed to escape from the premises or to be blown around the site

- ensure that all waste is collected and disposed of by an appropriately licensed waste disposal contractor

- wherever possible/practicable try to recycle/re-use waste materials

- crush cardboard boxes and other materials to reduce their bulk and the space required for their storage.

Fume and odour management checklist

Nasty niffs, whether on a small or industrial scale, can impact on quality of life. As such, you need to ensure that your business isn't having a negative effect on your neighbours.

FUME AND ODOUR MANAGEMENT

Do your processes create any fumes or odours? If so, you might need our **Fume and Odour Management Checklist**. This document will provide a template for a site audit to assess what fumes and odours you may be producing and it will also help you assess the likelihood of it causing a nuisance. As this can be quite a difficult exercise, we've added some tips for avoiding fume and odour problems on site. These should help you identify the source and suggest some possible solutions. Unlike waste and dust management, you may need to consider employing a consultant air monitoring company to test any emissions you're creating. This will ensure that you're not creating any harmful fumes that could cause health problems.

FUME AND ODOUR MANAGEMENT CHECKLIST

Company name:	Ref. no:		
Site location/address:	Site manager/responsible person:		
	Site manager contact details:		
Type of assessment:	❑ Routine	❑ Reactive	❑ Other

Environmental conditions				
Prevailing wind direction:	❑ North ❑ NE	❑ East ❑ NW	❑ South ❑ SE	❑ West ❑ SW
Average wind speed:	. . . . mph			
Maximum wind speed:	. . . . mph			
Weather conditions:	❑ Dry ❑ Overcast	❑ Wet ❑ Sunny	❑ Raining	
Location of persons affected:				

Site description:
Origin/source of fumes/odours generation: *(i.e. manufacturing processes, waste deposits, burning of waste, construction work, vehicular movements, etc.)*
Type of fumes/odours: *(i.e. smoke from chimneys, bonfires, exhaust fumes, manufacturing processes, treatment plants, etc.)*
Duration/timing: *(i.e. continuous, intermittent, sporadic, etc.)*
Details of control measures: *(i.e. filters, exhaust ventilation, dilution, chemical treatment, extraction, etc.)*
Details of any further action needed:
Additional comments:

Tips for avoiding fume/odour problems on site:

The checklist below can be used to minimise fume and odour problems on site:

- carry out a walk-through survey to identify potential sources of odour and fumes

- are there manufacturing/treatment processes or other equipment giving off harmful gases, fumes or odours?

- are separate exhaust ventilation systems provided where necessary?

- does the exhaust system vent away from neighbouring properties/premises where it could otherwise cause a nuisance?

- is ozone added to the air-conditioning system to "sweeten" the air?

- are biocides added to the system to control growth of micro-organisms?

- is there a kitchen or canteen where cooking is carried out and from which odours may emanate?

- are oil-fired boilers, appliances and other installations properly maintained and operating efficiently without creating dark smoke or plumes?

- is the burning of waste on site prohibited?

- are all septic tanks and treatment plants properly maintained and operated to prevent odours being generated?

- are chemicals and other substances with the potential to generate fumes/odours stored correctly?

- are skips and waste containers covered?

Noise management checklist

Making too much noise is a sure-fire way of upsetting your neighbours. As such, you need to identify where noise is being created and take steps to reduce levels where possible.

NOISE MANAGEMENT

Noisy neighbours are the classic example of a nuisance. So to help you avoid being one of them use our **Noise Management Checklist** to assess the source of any noise, how often it's likely to occur and potential ways of reducing the impact on your neighbours. The second part of our document includes tips for avoiding excessive noise with an on site guidance sheet. It provides some useful ways to prevent a problem occurring. If you identify a significant problem, we'd suggest you employ a noise consultant to carry out a full noise assessment of your site.

NOISE MANAGEMENT CHECKLIST

Company name:	Ref. no:			
Site location/address:	Site manager/responsible person:			
	Site manager contact details:			
Type of assessment:	❏ Routine	❏ Reactive	❏ Other	

Environmental conditions

Prevailing wind direction:	❏ North ❏ East ❏ South ❏ West ❏ NE ❏ NW ❏ SE ❏ SW
Average wind speed:	. . . . mph
Maximum wind speed:	. . . . mph
Weather conditions:	❏ Dry ❏ Wet ❏ Raining ❏ Overcast ❏ Sunny
Location of persons affected:	

Site description:

Origin/source of noise generation:
(i.e. manufacturing processes, construction work, vehicular movements etc.)

Type of noise:
(i.e. constant low or high level din, loud bangs etc.)

Duration/timing:
(i.e. continuous, intermittent, sporadic etc.)

Details of control measures:
(i.e. noise screens / barriers, silencers / mufflers etc.)

Details of any further action needed:

Additional comments:

Tips for avoiding noise problems on site:

The checklist below can be used to minimise noise on site:

- where practicable, carry out noisy fabrication or manufacturing works off site or in a less sensitive area

- keep noisy plant away from public areas

- adopt working hours to restrict noise activity to certain periods of the day and arrange delivery times to suit the area

- route delivery/construction vehicles to take account of the need to reduce noise and vibration, keep roads well maintained to avoid unnecessary noise caused by potholes etc.

- where possible, combine deliveries and have fewer, larger deliveries, rather than smaller, more frequent ones

- careful selection of plant is essential when noise is important (BS 5228 provides guidance)

- use only plant conforming to relevant standards and directives on emissions

- avoid older plant; although this is legal, it may be noisier and dirtier

- operate plant properly

- shut down plant when not in use or introduce a "no idling" policy

- maintain plant well

- if possible use noise screening/barriers

- monitor noise on site.

Chapter 4

Noise reduction
and control

Nuisance noise reduction and control policy and procedure

If you can foresee that noise may create a nuisance, it's worth having a formal policy in place, which sets out what you will do to manage it. This will be a clear indicator that you've recognised the potential for a problem and are prepared to address it. It's just the sort of thing an inspector will be looking for if they visit.

NUISANCE NOISE REDUCTION AND CONTROL

To help you identify the legal implications, understand the terminology and ascertain possible sources of noise, use our **Nuisance Noise Reduction and Control Policy and Procedure**. The policy section of the document can be amended to fit your business. It gives a clear indication to your staff, and possibly your clients and neighbours, that you've recognised noise to be a potential problem, you're aware of the legal implications and that you're going to do something about it.

THE PROCEDURE

This provides guidance on how to establish if nuisance noise is actually a problem and, if it is, what actions should be taken. It also details what needs to be recorded and what is involved in carrying out a basic nuisance noise assessment, together with the requirements for more in-depth noise monitoring studies.

NUISANCE NOISE REDUCTION AND CONTROL
POLICY AND PROCEDURE

1. General statement

It is our policy to ensure that disturbance and nuisance noise arising from our operations are kept to an acceptable level. The primary object is to ensure that nuisance noise is controlled and minimised where practicable. Whilst the basic principles outlined within this document should be applied to all works, particular reference should be made to ensuring that nuisance noise does not cause a disturbance during non-work hours.

Noise is essentially unwanted sound. Noise levels above 55dB(A) are known to affect concentration levels and can cause unnecessary stress and disturbance to individuals and therefore have the potential to cause noise pollution and a statutory nuisance.

To help ensure we give proper consideration to our environmental management responsibilities, and to assist in the determination of the causes and consequences of nuisance noise, all staff are expected to abide by the following procedures and co-operate with management in the execution of this Policy.

2. Legal position

There is a substantial amount of legislation governing the control of noise, including the **Control of Pollution Act 1974**, the **Environmental Protection Act 1990**, the **Noise and Statutory Nuisance Act 1993**, the **Noise Act 1996**, and the **Pollution Prevention and Control (England and Wales) Regulations 2000**. The main areas of enforcement for nuisance noise include:

Noise from commercial or industrial premises

Nuisance caused by noise from commercial or industrial premises such as shops or factories is dealt with under sections 79-82 of the **Environmental Protection Act 1990**.

Entertainment noise

Public places used for entertainment require a licence from the local authority. This licence will detail restrictions on noise in order to limit its impact on local residents.

If a noise nuisance is found to exist at a licensed premises, Environmental Health Officers may contact the management informally to advise them of the problem and encourage them to take voluntary action to remedy the problem. If the noise persists then further action may be taken.

Where licensed premises have been the cause of a statutory nuisance this will generally be reported to the Licensing Board and may influence their decision to renew or grant further licences.

Construction site noise

Sections 60-61 of the **Control of Pollution Act 1974** enable Environmental Health Officers to impose conditions on the way in which work is carried out on construction sites to limit the noise impact on neighbouring properties.

Section 60 enables local authorities to restrict the timing and duration of works, as well as influencing the way they are carried out and the type of plant/equipment used. Alternatively, section 61 can be used by developers to agree pre-set noise levels and working methods etc.

If, however, developers fail to adhere to the agreed times, then Environmental Health Officers may use powers granted under the above legislation to enforce the necessary restrictions.

Audible intruder alarms

When an audible intruder alarm causes nuisance through repeated activation then an officer from the Pollution Control Section will visit the premises concerned. The officer will discuss options with the occupier of the premises for silencing the alarm. If the occupier fails to remedy the problem and the alarm still activates unnecessarily and it is witnessed by the officer, then an Abatement Notice will be served under the **Environmental Protection Act 1990**.

Noise from vehicles, machinery or equipment in a road

Nuisance caused by noise from vehicles e.g. car alarms, noisy car repairs, parked refrigerator vehicles etc. can be dealt with by the Pollution Control Section under sections 79-82 of the **Environmental Protection Act 1990**. In such cases, the Officers may serve an Abatement Notice on the person responsible.

3. Definitions

Abatement Notice. If your Environmental Health Officer assesses that a statutory nuisance exists or is likely to occur, the local authority is duty bound to serve an Abatement Notice. Abatement Notices can;

* require you to abate the nuisance, i.e. to lessen or reduce it
* prohibit or restrict the nuisance
* require you to carry out works or other steps to abate, restrict or remove the nuisance.

Nuisance noise. Nuisance noise must be, or likely to be, prejudicial to people's health or interfere with a person's legitimate use and enjoyment of land. This particularly applies to nuisance to neighbours in their homes and gardens.

Section 60. Section 60 of the **Control of Pollution Act 1974** gives local authorities the power to serve a notice imposing requirements as to the way in which building, construction, maintenance and demolition etc. works are to be carried out.

Section 61. Section 61 provides the facility for those carrying out such works to apply in advance for a consent detailing how the works are to be carried out, thereby making themselves immune from action on noise grounds providing they are complying with the terms of the consent.

4. Management of nuisance noise

When considering the potential for nuisance noise, the number and location of residential and other noise sensitive properties likely to be affected needs to be considered relevant to the location and type of noise being generated.

When carrying out certain activities, such as building and construction, the use of heavy plant and equipment is unavoidably very noisy. It is therefore recognised that there are constraints to reducing the effects of nuisance noise in such instances. Consequently, placing restrictions on the working hours can be the most practicable option for limiting the impact on local residents and businesses.

Notwithstanding the above, it is important when considering potential noise reduction and control strategies, to establish all potential sources and locations of noise.

Potential sources can include:
- workshop machinery
- manufacturing plant/equipment
- large glass washers
- fire/burglar alarms
- air conditioning equipment
- power tools
- plant and equipment
- traffic movements
- loading/unloading of vehicles
- grounds maintenance equipment
- freezers
- pumping equipment
- construction/building work
- reversing alarms.

Potential locations where noise may be generated include:

- workshops
- kitchens
- animal houses
- construction sites
- entertainment venues
- car parks
- delivery areas
- waste storage areas.

Where potential noise issues are identified, further investigation and monitoring work should be carried out in order to assess the extent and impact of the noise on neighbouring properties. The undertaking of noise assessments of this type is a specialist activity and should be carried out by a "competent person".

However, where disturbance from noise is obvious, or has been confirmed through additional monitoring and noise surveys, steps should be taken to eliminate or minimise the effects before enforcement action is taken. The use of the following measures should be considered:

- use of alternative/less noisy plant/equipment
- scheduling noisy works to occur at less sensitive times
- carrying out noisy works at remote locations away from neighbouring properties
- use of low noise/silenced plant and equipment
- ensuring all plant and equipment is properly maintained and serviced
- use of acoustic screens.

Noise monitoring and assessment
policy and procedure

If you've recognised that noise may be an issue, the next step is to assess and monitor the noise levels. Having a formal policy and procedure in place will help your staff to identify if there's a problem and, most importantly, what they should be doing to manage it.

NOISE REDUCTION AND CONTROL

Whatever the nature of your business, you need to ensure that you aren't creating noise that's going to cause a nuisance. To do this, you'll need to make an assessment of potential noise sources and the possible impact these sources might have. To assist you, use our **Noise Monitoring and Assessment Policy and Procedure** document.

Note. If your operation is in a remote location, with no one likely to be affected by your works, then you aren't likely to be creating a nuisance. However, if your operations are in the middle of a housing estate, your neighbours are probably going to take a keener interest in what you're doing and what effect your operations are having on them.

Tip. Use our **Noise Monitoring Record Sheet** to record your assessment.

NOISE MONITORING AND ASSESSMENT
POLICY AND PROCEDURE

1. General statement

Where the generation of nuisance noise from our operations has been identified, our objective is to ensure that all such noise is controlled and minimised where practicable. In order to achieve this, noise monitoring will be carried out.

The results of any monitoring are used to highlight the location and cause of potential nuisance noise from our operations and activities.

To help ensure we give proper consideration to our environmental management responsibilities, and to assist in the determination of the causes and consequences of nuisance noise, all staff are expected to abide by the following procedures and co-operate with management in the execution of this Policy.

2. Definitions

L_{Aeq}. Refers to the "equivalent" average sound level measured using the A-weighting which is most sensitive to speech intelligibility frequencies of the human ear.

Nuisance noise. Nuisance noise must be, or likely to be, prejudicial to people's health or interfere with a person's legitimate use and enjoyment of land. This particularly applies to nuisance to neighbours in their homes and gardens.

Trigger level. The noise level at which additional actions or control measures should be implemented to limit or reduce the effects of nuisance noise.

Noise meter. Electronic device for the measurement and recording of sound levels.

Noise receptor. Location, typically a neighbouring property or premises, at which nuisance noise is heard. These are the locations where the level of noise is most important.

3. Monitoring procedure

All noise monitoring should be carried out by a competent person using a hand-held or tripod mounted integrating sound level meter to calculate noise levels at specific locations and at known times of the day. Noise meters used for monitoring purposes should comply with BS EN 60804 Type 2 specification, as required by BS5228: Noise and Vibration Control on Construction and Open Sites: Part 1:1997. This document provides good general guidance when considering the effects of nuisance noise and can be used as a basis of good practice in many different environments.

Before using noise monitoring equipment, ensure that it is fully charged, in a good state of repair, working correctly and has a valid calibration certificate. Noise levels should always be monitored at multiple locations around a site, approximately 1.2 - 1.5 metres above ground level, and in locations free from potential acoustic screens and subject to sound reflections.

Local weather conditions can greatly affect the results obtained during noise monitoring exercises. It is therefore important to ensure that all such environmental conditions are recorded as accurately as possible on the Noise Monitoring Record Sheet.

The duration of any noise monitoring shall be no less than five minutes at each location. Noise monitoring should be carried out various times throughout the working day in order to capture sufficient data on all potential sources of noise. The data should be recorded in terms of five minute "A" weighted $L_{eq.}$ If the recorded noise levels exceed the agreed trigger level this should be recorded on the Noise Monitoring Record Sheet and further monitoring should be instigated to assess the potential affects of nuisance noise beyond the boundaries of the company's site.

Where the noise trigger level has been exceeded, supplementary monitoring should be carried out to establish the extent of any potential nuisance noise on neighbouring properties. In such cases the duration of monitoring should be extended to a period of not less than one hour, with the noise monitoring being undertaken in a suitable position either at the boundary of the site or beyond the boundary closer to any potentially sensitive receptors of the noise.

Where the results of the additional monitoring indicate that nuisance noise may be a potential problem, remedial measures should be instigated to reduce and control its extent.

4. Reporting requirements

The results of all noise monitoring should be accurately recorded and documented on a Noise Monitoring Record Sheet. All pertinent information including local weather conditions, details of all activities being carried out on and off site, the time and duration of the monitoring and any remedial actions should all be recorded.

Copies of the record sheets should be maintained for future reference. The information contained in the record sheets can help to illustrate that we have taken a proactive approach to the management of nuisance noise.

Noise monitoring record sheet

The only way of identifying whether your site is creating excessive noise is to complete a full survey, carry out monitoring and record your results. As this will involve the use of specialist noise equipment, it will usually need to be completed by a competent consultant.

THE EVIDENCE

Although many businesses are accused of being noisy, when a survey and monitoring is carried out they're often able to prove that it's not a statutory nuisance. Being able to do this is especially important if the local authorities get involved and threaten to issue a notice, which would mean work having to stop. Use our **Noise Monitoring Record Sheet** to keep the results of your survey.

Tip. The records must be as accurate and detailed as possible. Recording the exact time, location, wind speed and background noise is vital; failure to do this could invalidate your survey.

NOISE MONITORING RECORD SHEET

Monitoring location:					
Description of location:					
Date & time of monitoring:					
Duration of monitoring:					
Type of noise meter/serial number:		**Last calibration date:**			
Type of monitoring:	Continuous/Spot checks/Peak levels/Personal/Other:				
Reason for monitoring:	Routine/Random/Reactive (following complaint)				
Weather conditions:	Rainy/Sunny/ Windy/Cloudy	**Wind direction/ speed:**			
Measurement results: **L90 (dB(A))**					
L10 (dB(A))					
Leq (dB(A))					
Peak level					
Trigger level to initiate action:		**Trigger level exceeded**	Yes/No		
Major noise sources during the monitoring:	Building work		On-site traffic		
	Air conditioning plant	Deliveries	Manufacturing processes		
	Other:				
Other sources of noise during the monitoring:	Off-site traffic	Air traffic	Neighbouring premises		
	Road works	Animal noise	Schools		
	Other:				
Comments:					

Guidance note - noise assessment and control

Unwanted noise and can cause problems with neighbours in addition to the more obvious risks to staff health. Our guidance note provides an introduction to the topic of environmental noise.

WHAT'S COVERED?

Our **Guidance Note - Noise Assessment and Control** sets out background information on noise nuisance including a summary of key legislation and details of penalties and enforcement practice. It goes on to explain briefly how an initial assessment can be made to determine whether there is a noise nuisance and also highlights key points of detailed noise monitoring which may be required. The final part of our document outlines the main ways in which noise can be controlled, helping you to identify the most practical options available. Use our guidance note to brief managers on the issues around noise on site, the likely consequences of neighbours' complaints and the options for noise reduction.

GUIDANCE NOTE -
NOISE ASSESSMENT AND CONTROL

Introduction

Noise is essentially unwanted sound. Noise can lead to hearing damage in extreme circumstances, but at even at low levels it may cause a nuisance both within and beyond the boundaries of the workplace. Noise which creates a nuisance is known as environmental noise.

Where it is determined that environmental noise may constitute a potential nuisance to neighbours, a noise assessment should be carried out. This guidance note focuses on the assessment and control of environmental noise as opposed to noise hazards. It is worth bearing in mind however, that noise which causes a nuisance to neighbours is likely to cause distraction and irritation to staff, at the very least.

Legislation

Under common law it is a civil wrong to create a nuisance, i.e. disrupt a person's right of quiet enjoyment of their property. In addition to the common law there are various pieces of legislation on the topic. For example:

Clean Neighbourhoods and Environment Act 2005. Introduces controls over noise and other nuisances and amends the **Noise Act 1996**, so that it applies to licensed premises at night, as well as dwellings.

Environmental Protection Act 1990 Part III. Gives local authorities powers to deal with a wide range of statutory nuisances including noise.

Anti-social Behaviour Act 2003. Applies controls over noisy premises, amongst other nuisances.

Control of Noise (Codes of Practice for Construction and Open Sites) (England) Order 2002. This Order approves four British Standards for methods of minimising noise and vibration from construction and open sites in England - BS5228 parts 1, 3, 4 and 5.

Noise Act 1996. Permits certain levels of noise and explains how levels will be measured and enforced.

There are also various regulations which control the noise emission standards of new appliances, equipment, tyres and machinery. Meanwhile, planning, licence or environmental permit conditions may apply at individual premises, resulting in certain noise levels being permitted or not permitted as appropriate.

If the local authority is satisfied that a statutory nuisance exists, is likely to occur or recur, they must serve an abatement notice. This may require the activity causing the nuisance to stop altogether, or that good practice is adopted to prevent a nuisance. There is a right of appeal within 21 days of the notice being served.

Complainants are also able to pursue independent action through the magistrates' court to seek an abatement notice.

Industrial, trade and business premises, as well as relevant sports premises, may use as a defence upon appeal or against prosecution, the proof that "best practicable means" were used to prevent or counteract the effects of a nuisance.

When the nuisance arises on industrial, trade or business premises, the maximum fine for failing to comply with an abatement notice is £20,000.

Noise assessment techniques

Noise is measured in decibels (dB). A weighting system has been developed which relates the noise level to the normal human hearing range. This is known as A weighting and is written as dB(A).

There are various permitted levels according to time of day and depending on whether the noise occurs in England, Scotland or Wales. A common theme is that, except where underlying noise levels are very low, the noise received in the neighbouring dwelling should not exceed 10dB(A) above the underlying noise level.

An initial nuisance noise assessment is used to determine whether or not a nuisance noise may exist. Any specific local circumstances should be considered first, e.g. whether the noise levels are within licence/ planning/ permit conditions for the premises. In terms of a defence against statutory noise nuisance allegations, it should be identified whether the "best practicable means" are being employed to prevent the noise nuisance. Where the first stage identifies a potential issue, it may then be necessary to monitor and define the actual level of noise being generated.

Initial nuisance noise assessment

The following techniques can be used to determine if a nuisance noise problem exists:

- review of complaints from staff and neighbours

- review of enforcement action/correspondence from local Environmental Health Officers

- use of noise monitoring equipment to measure actual sound levels from each noise source, where possible, taking such readings within neighbouring premises

- evaluation of rules applying to the site, in particular environmental permits, planning conditions or licence conditions and an evaluation as to whether requirements appear to be met.

Noise monitoring

Where the initial assessment identifies a potential nuisance noise, or a noise level above an agreed trigger level, then more detailed monitoring should be implemented to identify the noise source and levels.

All noise monitoring should be carried out by a "competent person" using a calibrated noise meter and the findings of the monitoring should be recorded and thoroughly assessed to determine if further action to reduce or eliminate the noise is required. Any programme of environmental noise monitoring should take into account the recommendations of BS 7445.

Noise control

The preferred method of controlling nuisance noise should follow the general hierarchy of control in order to eliminate or control the noise to acceptable levels. This hierarchy can be summarised as:

(i) Control the noise at source

Where practicable, the replacement or termination of noisy processes, activities or equipment is likely to be the most effective means of noise reduction. Suppliers of new equipment should be able to provide noise emission data based on anticipated noise characteristics within an average workplace. The use of a Low Noise Hire and Purchasing Policy will assist in this respect by ensuring that all new equipment with the potential for generating nuisance noise is properly assessed before it is purchased.

(ii) Noise reduction techniques

Where the generation of noise is unavoidable, measures should be considered that would reduce it to acceptable levels, by, for example:

- avoiding metal-on-metal impacts, e.g. by lining metal chutes with abrasion-resistant rubber, and reducing the height of drops

- using dampening, e.g. rubber bushes, to reduce vibration caused by plant and machinery

- ensuring all plant, machinery and equipment is correctly set up and maintained

- adding enclosures to contain and house noisy equipment and processes

- fitting silencers to air exhausts and blowing nozzles

- erecting noise attenuation barriers and screens to block the direct path of the sound

- repositioning noisy processes away from potentially sensitive receptors

- limiting the time of day and duration during which noisy processes/tasks are permitted to be carried out.

(iii) Information, instruction and training

Where nuisance noise is considered to be an issue, those in charge of, and responsible for, the noise-generating activities are to be informed and instructed about the effects of the noise on others and the controls that should be instigated to limit and/or reduce its effects.

(iv) Monitoring and recording

The suitability and effectiveness of all noise reduction and control measures should be regularly reviewed and monitored to ensure that they are operating correctly and efficiently. Records should be made of the actions taken to control/reduce noise levels, together with records of any complaints about nuisance noise and any additional noise monitoring that may be carried out from time-to-time.

Initial nuisance noise assessment

If you have a noise problem, a full-blown noise assessment carried out by experts needn't be your first step. Before you do this, you should complete a basic assessment.

MAKING AN ASSESSMENT

If you've had a complaint about noise on your site, or even if you want to carry out a simple assessment of noise levels just in case, you don't need to employ the services of an expert as a first step. All you will need is our **Initial Nuisance Noise Assessment** document.

Note. This is a very simple assessment and doesn't qualify as a full noise survey. If, when completing this survey, it's identified that noise levels might be high enough to be a nuisance, a full noise survey should be completed.

INITIAL NUISANCE NOISE ASSESSMENT

Item	Response	Comments
Reason for assessment:		
Brief description of the type and duration of the noise:		
Weather conditions:		
Location of the noise:		
Source of the noise (if known):		
Time when noise is generated:		
Operations during which noise is noticed:		
Is the noise related to any specific activity:		
Does the noise affect neighbouring properties:		
State those affected:		
Has this noise been reported previously:		
Conclusions:		
Actions:		
Assessment completed by:		Date:

Low noise hire and purchasing policy

Purchasing equipment that's noisy could create a problem that's both expensive and time consuming to solve. So if you adopt a policy of buying low noise equipment wherever possible, you'll minimise the potential amount of remedial work necessary.

Low noise hire and purchasing policy

To help ensure that those responsible for purchasing and hiring equipment are fully aware of their responsibilities and the consequences that their actions may have on others, the **Low Noise Hire and Purchasing Policy** can be implemented to provide guidance. The adoption of this policy can also help to demonstrate to the enforcement authorities that your organisation is committed to maintaining the highest environmental standards.

Note. In addition to preventing potential statutory nuisance issues, purchasing low noise equipment will also go some way to covering your health and safety duty of care imposed by the **Control of Noise at Work Regulations 2005**. For further information on these Regulations visit: http://www.legislation.gov. uk/uksi/2005/1643/contents/made

LOW NOISE
HIRE AND PURCHASING POLICY

As part of our strategy for minimising the effects of both nuisance, and hazardous noise, a Low Noise Hire and Purchasing Policy has been developed. The purpose of this Policy is to introduce a positive and cost-effective approach to the control and reduction of workplace and nuisance noise issues.

By choosing to purchase or hire quieter plant, equipment and machinery, significant savings can be made on subsequent noise-reduction measures once the equipment has been installed or is in use. This Policy requires all those with responsibility for the purchase, hire or specification of suitable plant, equipment or machinery to:

- consider the effects that new or replacement plant, machinery or other equipment may have on the generation of both workplace and nuisance noise

- ensure that noise levels as low as realistically possible are specified to suppliers and within appropriate tender documents, and that suppliers are made aware of their legal obligations

- discuss with suppliers what the requirements for the equipment are and what the likely noise levels will be when used for its intended purpose

- compare and contrast the manufacturer's specified noise levels for equipment from different suppliers

- purchase/hire equipment from suppliers who can demonstrate a low-noise design with noise control measures featured as standard and not as a costly optional extra

- maintain an audit trail of the decisions taken when selecting equipment to help demonstrate that the company has complied with its statutory obligations with regards to reducing workplace and nuisance noise

- discuss with suppliers installation requirements and arrangements to ensure that the equipment is operated correctly

- discuss maintenance arrangements with suppliers to ensure that the equipment continues operating efficiently and does not get louder over time.

Furthermore, under the **Health and Safety at Work etc. Act 1974** and the **Supply of Machinery (Safety) Regulations 1992** (as amended), suppliers of machinery must:

- design and construct machinery so that the noise produced is as low as possible

- provide information about the noise the machine produces under actual working conditions.

Through implementing this policy, the risks associated with the generation of nuisance noise will be greatly minimised.

Register of environmental legislation -

noise and nuisance issues

This part of our Register of Environmental Legislation covers noise and nuisance issues. Nuisance covers a wide range of problems including fly tipping and grafitti.

WHY YOU NEED OUR REGISTER

It's useful to hold a **Register of Environmental Legislation** even if you are not required to do so (you may need to if you're ISO14001 certified). Having a register enables you to systematically identify which legislation applies to your business and how. It can also be useful if you're inspected by the Environment Agency or to satisfy clients during vetting procedures.

NOISE AND NUISANCE

Our register is pre-filled with the most commonly applicable legislation in England on the topic of noise and nuisance. It includes the title of the legislation, a brief summary of its purpose, the details of the regulator and a final column for you to complete details of what you've done to comply. Although the fourth column is provided for you to complete details of your own arrangements, we've given some examples to lead the way.

REGISTER OF ENVIRONMENTAL LEGISLATION - NOISE AND NUISANCE ISSUES

Introduction

The Environmental Management Standard ISO 14001 recommends that each organisation "establishes and maintains a procedure to identify and have access to legal and other requirements to which the organisation subscribes, that are applicable to the environmental aspects of its activities, products or services."

It is the purpose of this register of environmental legislation to demonstrate compliance with this standard.

Noise and statutory nuisance

(**Note.** *This table lists the most commonly applicable legislation relating to noise and nuisance. Delete and amend as required and complete the "Aspects of activities affected" column as appropriate to your business.*)

Legislation	Summary	Regulator	Aspects of activities affected (Describe how and why the legislation affects you. Refer to associated internal documents)
Clean Neighbourhoods and Environment Act 2005	Introduces controls over noise, litter, grafitti, fly posting, the display of advertisements, abandoned vehicles, abandoned shopping trolleys etc. Classifies artificial lighting and insects as statutory nuisances. Amends the Noise Act 1996, so that it applies to licensed premises at night, as well as dwellings.	Local authorities	*e.g. We have taken steps to ensure compliance with these regulations in our noise emissions and advertising strategy.*

Legislation	Summary	Regulator	Aspects of activities affected (Describe how and why the legislation affects you. Refer to associated internal documents)
Environmental Protection Act 1990 Part III	Gives local authorities powers to deal with a wide range of statutory nuisances including noise and "any accumulation or deposit which is prejudicial to health or a nuisance".	Local authorities	*e.g. We use the best practicable means to control noise in the form of low noise emitting machinery and sound insulation.*
Anti-social Behaviour Act 2003	Extends powers for local authorities to clean up the environment, and applies controls over noisy premises, advertisements and waste.	Local authorities	

Legislation	Summary	Regulator	Aspects of activities affected (Describe how and why the legislation affects you. Refer to associated internal documents)
Control of Noise (Codes of Practice for Construction and Open Sites) (England) Order 2002	Under section 71 of the Control of Pollution Act 1974, the Secretary of State may give guidance on appropriate methods for minimising noise and vibration by approving codes of practice. These include building and roadworks, demolition, dredging and other works of engineering construction. This Order approves four British Standards for methods of minimising noise and vibration from construction and open sites in England - BS5228 parts 1,3,4 and 5.	N/A	*e.g. We apply approved codes for noise control when undertaking construction work.*
Environmental Noise (England) Regulations 2006 as amended 2009	Requires the government to identify noise sources for strategic noise maps and noise action areas to be drawn up for covering large areas of population, major roads, railways and airports.	N/A	

Legislation	Summary	Regulator	Aspects of activities affected (Describe how and why the legislation affects you. Refer to associated internal documents)
Household Appliances (Noise Emission) Regulations 1990 as amended 1994	Sets airborne noise levels for appliances and bans the marketing of appliances that do not conform to these standards.	Local authorities - Trading Standards	*e.g. We are not involved in the marketing of appliances.*
Noise Emission in the Environment by Equipment for Use Outdoors Regulations 2001 as amended 2001 and 2005	Establishes maximum noise levels for equipment used outdoors, mainly in construction and land maintenance, such as generators, lawn mowers, compaction machines and concrete breakers.	Local authorities - Trading Standards	*e.g. We ensure that equipment purchased conforms with CE requirements and includes information on noise emission. This information is taken into account within risk assessments.*
Road Vehicles (Construction and Use) (Amendment) Regulations 2010	Requires that tyres fitted to certain vehicles are marked with an S mark to show that they comply with the noise emission requirements of EU Directives.	Local authorities - Trading Standards	*e.g. Our tyres are sourced from reputable suppliers.*
Common Law	Under common law it is a civil wrong to create a nuisance, i.e. disrupt a person's right of quiet enjoyment of their property.	Individuals have the right to sue	*e.g. We take into account the rights of our neighbours in the way that we manage site appearance, litter, potential spillages and vehicle movements.*

Chapter 5

Waste management

Guidance note - duty of care

Waste is a dirty business at the best of times, but not complying with one of the many laws that control waste disposal in the UK can cost you dearly. To help you decipher these laws, why not use our guidance note?

WHAT IS WASTE?

The definition of "waste" is wide ranging and is used to cover everything that is effectively unwanted; this ranges from normal domestic waste to commercial/industrial waste, builders' waste, radioactive and other hazardous wastes.

YOUR DUTY OF CARE

Under the **Environmental Protection Act 1990**, a duty of care was introduced with regards to the management and disposal of waste. The duty of care sets out specific requirements and obligations for those who produce, transport and dispose of waste. We've summarised the main points in our **Guidance Note - Duty of Care**, to help you identify what it means to your business and how you can ensure that you comply with it.

GUIDANCE NOTE - DUTY OF CARE

Every organisation is required to take all reasonable steps to keep and dispose of their waste safely. If waste is passed on to a third party, it is essential that checks are made to ensure they are authorised to accept and can transport, recycle or dispose of it safely. Failing to comply with this requirement can lead to an unlimited fine.

These requirements were introduced by s.34 of Environmental Protection Act 1990 (EPA). Under sections 34 and 47 of the EPA it is an offence if you fail to ensure that your waste is disposed of correctly. The duty applies to any trading persons who produce or import, keep or store, transport, treat or dispose of any waste materials. It also applies if you act as a waste broker and arrange for any of these activities to be carried out.

What is waste?

Waste can be anything you (or your organisation) intend to dispose of, are required to dispose of or actually dispose of. Material being recovered, e.g. being prepared for re-use, also counts as waste.

Examples of waste might include packaging, waste paper, and construction waste such as rubble and waste materials.

Controlled waste

This is household, commercial or industrial waste. It can be from a domestic property, school, university, hospital, residential or nursing home, shop, office, factory, workshop, building site or any other trade or business. It may be solid or liquid, scrap metal or a scrap car. It does not have to be hazardous or toxic to be a controlled waste.

Domestic household waste

If the waste originates from a domestic property, the duty of care does not apply to you. But if the waste is not from the house you live in, for example if it is waste from your workplace or waste from someone else's house, the duty of care does apply.

What counts as hazardous waste?

Waste is considered "hazardous" if it is harmful to human health or the natural environment. **Note.** The phrase "**hazardous waste**" is used to describe this type of waste in England, Wales and Northern Ireland. In Scotland, the phrase "**special waste**" is used instead.

Examples of hazardous waste include:

- lead-acid batteries

- fluorescent light tubes

- electrical equipment containing hazardous components, such as cathode ray tubes in televisions

- waste oils

- solvents

- discarded chemicals

- asbestos.

You can check whether waste is considered hazardous at http://www.environment-agency.gov.uk/business/topics/waste/32200.aspx.

Complying with the duty of care

Every business that produces (or imports, carries, keeps, treats, recovers or disposes of) waste is under a **duty of care** to manage this safely and legally. This involves:

- storing waste in accordance with regulations

- stopping their waste from escaping their control and causing pollution or harm to anyone

- sorting and segregating waste as required

- making sure that others who handle, recover or dispose of your waste are authorised to do so

- in the case of specific types of waste, complying with additional duties, e.g. developing waste management plans for large construction projects, receiving and processing returned batteries in the case of certain retailers etc., managing packaging waste in the case of producers.

Storing waste

Waste must always be protected and stored in order to prevent it from escaping from its container. Waste holders must safeguard against:

- corrosion

- scavenging/weather (cover it if it's at risk of blowing away)

- spillages/leaks.

Some wastes need to be separated from each other, e.g. you must not mix different types of hazardous waste, and you must not mix hazardous with non-hazardous waste or with materials that are not waste. For example, waste electrical and electronic equipment (WEEE) must be stored, collected, treated, reused, recovered or disposed of separately from any other waste your business produces.

There are also specific storage requirements for some wastes, such as animal by-products, waste vehicles, construction waste and radioactive waste.

If you are sending waste for disposal to a landfill, it must be pre-treated to minimise its impact on the environment. This is often as simple as separating the waste into different materials. You can either pay your waste contractor to do this or treat the waste yourself. Discuss the requirements and alternatives with your waste contractor.

Rules for disposing of hazardous waste

Certain businesses producing hazardous waste in England or Wales must register their premises with the Environment Agency before any waste is removed. However, there is an exemption which applies to producers of less than 500 kilograms of hazardous waste per year.

Hazardous waste producers in Northern Ireland and special waste producers in Scotland must pre-notify their enforcing authority (i.e. Northern Ireland Environment Agency/ SEPA) before it is moved.

In addition to the storage and segregation requirements mentioned earlier, there are some additional duties relating to hazardous waste. For example, you must:

- provide written instructions for your employees about how to store and dispose of the hazardous waste you produce

- draw up an inventory of all the hazardous waste on your premises in case the emergency services ever need it

- carry out a weekly inspection of hazardous waste containers

- ensure that the waste is transported correctly, complying with "dangerous goods" legislation

- check that the place receiving the waste is authorised to take it

- ensure a consignment note is completed for every load of hazardous waste transferred, and keep the notes for at least three years.

There are special rules about certain types of waste, so if you need to dispose of animal by-products, end of life vehicles, construction waste, waste batteries and accumulators or radioactive waste, you should seek additional information.

There are also additional rules for producers and distributors of electronic waste.

When giving your waste to a third party

If waste is given or passed on to another company or individual, check that they have the appropriate registration/authority to accept, transport and dispose of it. The waste must also be described in writing on a signed waste transfer note. These can be single notes or "season tickets" (to cover repeated transfers of the same type of waste to the same handler). A copy of each waste transfer note should be retained for a minimum period of two years.

When you take waste from someone else

If you accept waste from another party, it is essential to ensure that the law allows you to do so.

You also need to ensure that the person giving you the waste describes it in writing. You must fill in and sign a transfer note and retain a copy to demonstrate how you have discharged your duty of care.

Who has authority to take trade waste?

Registered waste carriers

Most carriers of waste have to be registered with the Environment Agency (EA) or the Scottish Environment Protection Agency (SEPA). Look at the carrier's certificate of registration or check with the EA/SEPA.

Holders of waste management licences

Some licences are valid only for certain kinds of waste or certain activities. Ask to see the licence. Check that the licence covers your kind of waste.

Documentation

An accurate description of the waste must be written on the transfer note. It must be completed and signed by both persons involved in the transfer and include:

- a description of the waste and how much there is

- the date and time of the transfer

- the names and addresses of both persons involved in the transfer.

If either person is a registered waste carrier, enclose the certificate number and the name of the EA office which issued the certificate.

Duty of care controlled waste
transfer note

When waste is taken from your site, a waste transfer note must be completed. It should identify the nature and quantity of the waste, and the location of the site it's being taken to. Never allow waste to be taken away without one.

RECORD OF COLLECTION

Our example **Duty of Care Controlled Waste Transfer Note** will help you see what information your business and the waste contractor must complete. All reputable waste contractors will assist in the completion of the transfer notes so that they also comply with the duty of care imposed on them as the registered waste contractor.

Tip. If a waste carrier doesn't want to use transfer notes, this is likely to indicate that the waste will be dumped illegally.

Tip. Always keep a copy of the document because if the waste is dumped illegally, it will be the only evidence you'll have to prove that you had complied with your duty of care to ensure that your waste is disposed of properly.

DUTY OF CARE CONTROLLED WASTE TRANSFER NOTE

Description of waste

1. Description of the waste being transferred:

2. European Waste Catalogue Code:

3. How is the waste contained?

Loose ❑   Sacks ❑   Skip ❑   Drum ❑

Other ❑   Please describe: . . . .

4. What is the quantity of waste? (number of drums, tonnes etc.):

Current holder of the waste (transferor)

Full name:. . . . .

Name and address of company: . . . .

Which of the following are you? (one or more boxes may apply)

❑ waste producer	❑ holder of waste management licence	licence no: . . . . issued by: . . . .
❑ waste importer	❑ exempt from waste management licensing	reason why: . . . .
❑ waste collection authority	❑ registered waste carrier	registration no: . . . . issued by: . . . .
❑ waste disposal authority (Scotland only)	❑ exempt from requirement to register	reason why: . . . .

Person collecting the waste (transferee)

Full name:

Name and address of company:

Which of the following are you? (one or more boxes may apply)

❑ waste collection authority	❑ authorised for transport purpose	specify purpose:. . . . . . .

❑ waste disposal authority (Scotland only)

❑ holder of waste management licence   licence no: . . . .
issued by: . . . .

❑ exempt from waste management licensing   reason why: . . . .

❑ registered waste carrier   registration no: . . . .
issued by: . . . .

❑ exempt from requirement to register   reason why: . . . .

Address of place of transfer:

. . . .
. . . .

Date of transfer:. . . . .

Time of transfer (for multiple loads give between dates): . . . .

Name and address of broker (if applicable):

. . . .
. . . .

	Transferor	**Transferee**
Signature:	. . . .	. . . .
Full name:	. . . .	. . . .
Representing:	. . . .	. . . .

Adapted from HMSO Publication "Waste Management The Duty of Care: A Code of Practice.

Guidance note - managing hazardous waste

Manufacturing, construction and pharmaceutical businesses are likely to produce hazardous waste, amongst many others. Hazardous waste can be anything from certain types of food waste, to chemicals, asbestos and more. Due to its nature it needs to be segregated from other waste.

MANAGING HAZARDOUS WASTE

To help you comply with the **Hazardous Waste Regulations 2005** and the **List of Waste Regulations 2005**, we've created a **Guidance Note - Managing Hazardous Waste**. This provides basic guidance on the Regulations and what you need to do to ensure that you comply with them.

GUIDANCE NOTE -
MANAGING HAZARDOUS WASTE

In April 2005, the Department for Environment, Food and Rural Affairs (DEFRA) issued two sets of regulations for England and Wales:

(i) **Hazardous Waste Regulations.** These Regulations control and track the movement of hazardous waste. On July 16 2005, they replaced the **Special Waste Regulations 1996**.

(ii) **List of Wastes Regulations.** These Regulations provide a classification of hazardous wastes, incorporating the EU hazardous waste list.

The definition of what is hazardous waste is wide ranging and covers everything from waste food, to fluorescent light tubes to asbestos. Waste is generally classed as hazardous if it contains substances or has properties that might make it harmful to human health or to the environment. For a definitive list of all hazardous wastes, please visit the following link, or contact the Environment Agency to discuss your situation:

http://www.opsi.gov.uk/si/si2005/20050895.htm

The **Hazardous Waste Regulations** introduced a more manageable system for the tracking the movement of hazardous wastes and have also restricted the mixing of wastes, requiring their separation wherever possible.

Hazardous waste producers have a legal duty to register their premises with the Environment Agency. The producer must submit quarterly reports. Regular audits to ensure legal compliance can be expected.

Is your business likely to be affected?

Your business is likely to be classed as producing hazardous waste if it's involved in waste producing activities such as construction, demolition and asbestos removal, or carries out operations that may result in compositional change of your waste.

The threshold for exempt premises, i.e., domestic properties, shops, offices and hospitals, is the production of 200kg of hazardous waste in a twelve-month period. All industrial premises producing hazardous waste have to be registered with the Environment Agency, regardless of the amount produced.

Transporting hazardous wastes

Whenever hazardous wastes are to be removed or transported, the producer or holder must prepare a consignment note. There are two types of consignment note - one for single and another for multiple movements.

A copy of the consignment note should be retained by each of the parties who either produce, store or handle the waste. Before accepting the waste the carrier should check the consignment note and ensure that its description corresponds with what's being collected.

Producers of hazardous waste must retain: records of the quantity, nature, origin and, where relevant:

• the destination

• frequency of collection

• mode of transport and treatment of the waste.

Identification records for the carrier of each consignment of hazardous waste that leaves your premises also need to be kept in a register for at least three years.

On arriving at the waste disposal, transfer or recycling site, the paperwork should be handed to the person receiving the waste. At this point they have the right to reject the waste if:

• it doesn't conform with the paperwork or

• if the disposal site or transfer station is not authorised to take that particular category of waste or

• if no consignment note is available.

The person receiving the waste must also make a return of the completed consignment note within one month of the end of the quarter in which it was accepted. This assists with the management and recording of consignment notes. Use the attached Register of Hazardous Waste Consignment Notes to log and monitor the status of each note.

Consignment notes for multiple collections apply when a carrier collects more than one consignment of waste from different premises in a single journey. In these instances, a different format is to be used for the consignment.

Register of environmental legislation - waste

Having a professional-looking Register of Environmental Legislation is a good way of showing that you know what your doing. If you're a contracting organisation, it can help you to pass contractor vetting procedures.

WHY YOU NEED OUR REGISTER

The first step in most environmental management systems is usually to identify the legislation that applies and how. But even if you don't want to go for certification under ISO14001, it doesn't hurt to show that you know a bit about the waste legislation that affects you. Our **Register of Environmental Legislation** will show that you're up-to-date with the latest legal requirements and that you've carefully considered how they affect you. Part 1 lists the most commonly applicable waste legislation in England.

ADAPTING THE CONTENTS

After a short introduction the register includes a table with four columns:

1. Legislation

2. Summary

3. Regulator

4. Aspects of activities affected (Describe how and why the legislation affects you. Refer to associated internal documentation).

The first three columns are completed and the fourth is free for you to provide details of how the legislation affects your business and what you've done about it.

REGISTER OF ENVIRONMENTAL LEGISLATION - WASTE

Introduction

The Environmental Management Standard ISO 14001 recommends that each organisation "establishes and maintains a procedure to identify and have access to legal and other requirements to which the organisation subscribes, that are applicable to the environmental aspects of its activities, products or services."

It is the purpose of this register of environmental legislation to demonstrate compliance with this standard.

Part 1 Waste

(**Note.** *This table lists the most commonly applicable legislation relating to waste. Delete and amend as required and complete the "Impact" column as appropriate to your business.*)

Legislation	Summary	Regulator	Aspects of activities affected (Describe how and why the legislation affects you. Refer to associated internal documents)
Controlled Waste Regulations 1992 as amended	Defines household, industrial and commercial waste for waste management licensing purposes.	Environment Agency (EA)	
Environmental Protection Act 1990, Part II	Defines within England, Scotland and Wales the legal framework for duty of care for waste, contaminated land and statutory nuisance. Under Section 33 it is an offence to treat, keep or dispose of controlled waste without a waste management licence, or in a manner likely to cause pollution of the environment or harm to human health. Section 34 sets out a statutory duty of care for all those producing or dealing with waste.	EA	

Legislation	Summary	Regulator	Aspects of activities affected (Describe how and why the legislation affects you. Refer to associated internal documents)
Environmental Protection (Duty of Care) Regulations 1991 as amended	Imposes a duty of care on any person who imports, produces, carries, keeps, treats or disposes of controlled waste to ensure there is no unauthorised or harmful depositing, treatment or disposal of the waste. Those with a duty of care are required to prepare and retain written descriptions of waste and transfer notes. 2003 amendment allows waste collection authorities in England to serve notices on people required to keep written descriptions of waste and transfer notices, and to require them to produce such documents to the authority within a specified time.	EA	e.g. *We ensure that waste transfer notes contain a description of the waste and all parties in the transaction. Notes are kept for a minimum of two years. Waste is only transferred to an authorised waste carrier.* *See Waste Transfer Notes folder*
List of Wastes (England) Regulations 2005 as amended	Provides the European Waste Catalogue list of codes used to classify wastes. Minor corrections in 2005 amendment.	EA	

Legislation	Summary	Regulator	Aspects of activities affected (Describe how and why the legislation affects you. Refer to associated internal documents)
Environmental Permitting (England and Wales) Regulations 2007 (Replaced most previous waste management licensing legislation in England and Wales in 2008)	These Regulations underpin the whole of the waste management licensing system and their scope is being increased by phasing in new requirements. They introduced a system for environmental permits (and exemptions) for industrial activities and waste operations, including landfill and waste incineration, and set out the powers, functions and duties of the regulator.	EA	
Hazardous Waste (England and Wales) Regulations 2005 as amended (Replaced Special Waste Regulations 1996 as amended)	Details requirements for controlling and tracking the movement of hazardous waste and bans mixing different types of hazardous waste. 2009 amendment increased the maximum limit of hazardous waste that can be produced in any year without registering with the regulator from 200kg to 500kg.	EA	*e.g. We do produce hazardous waste, such as redundant computer equipment, but are under the threshold for registration. Any hazardous waste collected by licensed waste contractor.*

Legislation	Summary	Regulator	Aspects of activities affected (Describe how and why the legislation affects you. Refer to associated internal documents)
Control of Pollution (Amendment) Act 1989	Requires carriers of controlled waste to register with the Environment Agency or SEPA and outlines the penalties (including seizure and disposal) for vehicles shown to have been used for illegal waste disposal.	EA	
Controlled Waste (Registration of Carriers and Seizure of Vehicles) Regulations 1991	Introduced a registration system for carriers of controlled waste. Amended in 1998 to update procedures for registration.	EA	
Clean Neighbourhoods and Environment Act 2005	Introduced additional legislation on noise, litter, abandoned vehicles, fly tipping, and construction site waste. The focus is on local authority powers and local regulation.	Local authority	
Environment Act 1995	Established the Environment Agency and SEPA as the regulating bodies for contaminated land, abandoned mines, national parks, control of pollution, conservation of natural resources, conservation or enhancement of the environment, and fisheries.	EA	

Legislation	Summary	Regulator	Aspects of activities affected (Describe how and why the legislation affects you. Refer to associated internal documents)
Landfill Tax Regulations 1996 (as amended)	Established a system of taxation on wastes disposed of to landfill in order to promote a more sustainable approach to waste management. The cost per tonne of waste going to landfill increases each year. It's £40 per tonne as of Feb 2010 (inert wastes at £2.50).	HMRC	
Landfill (England and Wales) Regulations 2002	Set targets for reduction of biodegradable municipal waste to landfill, introduces classification for landfill sites, specifies that only treated wastes will be accepted and bans the disposal to landfill of specified wastes, e.g. liquids, tyres, hazardous, clinical waste and untreated waste. Hazardous wastes are only accepted at authorised landfill sites. Waste producers must ensure that alternative arrangements are made for the disposal of liquid wastes and ensure that solid, non-hazardous wastes are treated before they're disposed of.	EA	e.g. *We've ensured that the waste carrier is licensed and operates a treatment process on the waste prior to disposal. We know the landfill site to be used and have checked that it has the correct environmental permit to accept the type of waste we're disposing of.*

Legislation	Summary	Regulator	Aspects of activities affected (Describe how and why the legislation affects you. Refer to associated internal documents)
Waste Electrical and Electronic Equipment Regulations 2006 as amended	Aims to reduce the amount of waste electrical and electronic equipment (WEEE) sent to landfill. Require producers of EEE to register and cover the costs of collecting, treating, recovering and disposing of equipment when it reaches the end of its life. 2007 amendment encouraged prioritising re-use of whole appliances in the WEEE system. 2009 amendment altered the Producer Compliance Scheme approval process and simplified data reporting requirements.	EA	

Legislation	Summary	Regulator	Aspects of activities affected (Describe how and why the legislation affects you. Refer to associated internal documents)
Waste Batteries and Accumulators Regulations 2009	Set out rules for the collection, treatment and recycling of all types of batteries and accumulators (rechargeable batteries). Affects producers, sellers, distributors, waste treatment sites and waste battery exporters. From February 1 2010 retailers or distributors who sell more than 32kg of portable batteries and accumulators each year will have a responsibility to take them back in-store. They will have a right to make a collection request to an approved Battery Compliance Scheme, who must collect the waste batteries free of charge.	EA/Defra	
Producer Responsibility Obligations (Packaging Waste) Regulations 2007	Requires producers to recover and recycle packaging waste to achieve EU targets.	Trading Standards	
Packaging (Essential Requirements) Regulations 2003 as amended 2004, 2006, 2009	Set out essential requirements for packaging which apply to packaging producers, sellers and distributors, including enforcement, offences and penalties.	Trading Standards	

Legislation	Summary	Regulator	Aspects of activities affected (Describe how and why the legislation affects you. Refer to associated internal documents)
Site Waste Management Plans Regulations 2008	Requires the preparation of a site waste management plan for any construction projects with an estimated cost of over £300,000.	EA/ Local authority	
End of Life Vehicles Regulations 2003	Requires vehicle producers to set up collection, treatment and disposal systems to make sure that components in vehicles can be recovered, reused and recycled at the end of their life.	Vehicle Certification Agency	
End of Life Vehicles (Producer Responsibility) Regulations 2005	Requires vehicle producers to register and declare responsibility for vehicles they place on the market and apply for approval of their system of collecting vehicles.	Vehicle Certification Agency	
Waste Management (England and Wales) Regulations 2006	Extends controlled waste to cover mine, quarry and agricultural waste. Categorises waste as household, industrial or commercial. Bans householders from treating, keeping, disposing of controlled waste if it could pollute the environment.	EA	

Register of hazardous waste

consignment notes

Whenever hazardous waste is taken from a site, a consignment note must be completed. A record of all consignment notes must be kept by the waste producer.

KEEPING RECORDS

To help keep your records up-to-date, use our **Register of Hazardous Waste Consignment Notes**. On it you can record the type of waste you've sent off site, who it was sent to and when.

Tip. Make sure your records are as accurate as possible because in the event of your hazardous waste being dumped illegally, being able to prove that you complied with your duty of care could prevent you from being prosecuted.

REGISTER OF HAZARDOUS WASTE CONSIGNMENT NOTES

Hazardous waste premises number

Unique consignment note code - six-digit premises number (as above)/ five digit alphanumeric (e.g. HW001 or 00001)

Unique consignment note code	Number issued by	Date waste removed from site	Description of waste removed	Waste code	Name of carrier	Name of disposal site	Date copy of completed consignment note returned

Note: Copies of all Hazardous Waste Consignment Notes should be retained on site for a minimum of three years.

Guidance note - hazardous waste minimisation

Getting rid of waste is an expensive business; some estimates put the costs at approximately 4.5% of annual turnover. So to help minimise your bills and to cut the amount of hazardous waste being sent to landfill etc. you should look to minimise waste wherever you can.

HAZARDOUS WASTE MINIMISATION

The best way of managing waste is not to create any in the first place. Unfortunately this is usually impossible. To help you cut the amount of hazardous waste you produce, use our **Guidance Note - Hazardous Waste Minimisation**. Minimising and recycling waste doesn't only save money on the costs of waste collection and disposal, but you may also avoid the need to register with the Environment Agency.

GUIDANCE NOTE -
HAZARDOUS WASTE MINIMISATION

Given that the hazardous waste regulations have a 200kg threshold before a premises needs to be registered, there are now even more reasons for minimising the amount of hazardous waste that organisations produce.

Minimising hazardous waste at source can not only help your business to avoid the need to register your premises with the Environment Agency, but it can also help to reduce the ever-increasing costs associated with its treatment and disposal, as well as helping to demonstrate your organisation's green credentials.

General tips for minimising hazardous waste

Simply improving an organisation's housekeeping practices is often the easiest and least expensive way to reduce any form of waste, including hazardous waste. Companies should therefore assess all aspects of their operations and waste handling practices in order to ascertain where efficiencies and reductions in waste may be made. The following points can be used to assist in identifying potential ways of reducing the amount of hazardous waste produced by your organisation:

Procurement

- estimate and use only the amount of materials necessary for a job
- substitute hazardous materials with non-hazardous alternatives
- maintain accurate records of materials to prevent materials and supplies from spoiling or becoming outdated
- keep accurate records of material usage so that you can measure reductions in use
- when purchasing materials, request copies of the Material Safety Data Sheets so that you may assess its hazardous content
- inspect materials upon delivery, and immediately return unacceptable materials to the supplier
- if making a special order, purchase only the amount of material needed to do a job
- when buying new equipment, look for equipment that will minimise both the amount of hazardous materials used and the amount of waste produced.

On site housekeeping

- keep premises clean and tidy at all times
- eliminate leaks and spills through a proactive maintenance regime
- use drip trays and catch pots to collect oil/fuel drippings and return them to a tank
- segregate hazardous and non-hazardous wastes for recycling
- encourage staff to regularly clean up waste material and dispose of it correctly.

Site waste management plan
(less than £500k)

A Site Waste Management Plan (SWMP) provides a structure for waste control and disposal at all stages during a construction project.

WHAT ARE THEY FOR?

Typically, an SWMP will help to identify:

• **who** will be responsible for resource management on site

• **what** types of waste will be generated on site

• **how** the waste will be managed - will it be reduced, reused or recycled

• **which** contractors will be used to ensure the waste is correctly recycled or disposed of responsibly and legally

• **how** the quantity of waste generated from the project will be measured.

USEFUL TOOL

Our completed **Site Waste Management Plan (Less than 500k)** will become a useful tool that shows how resources have been used and waste managed on your construction site, giving you valuable information for the future. It can help your business avoid prosecution by making sure all waste leaving site ends up at the right place. It also could help to cut costs. Remember that the information input to the SWMP will need to be developed to suit your particular project to make it work.

Note. SWMPs only affect anyone planning a construction project costing more than £300,000 in England.

SITE WASTE MANAGEMENT PLAN (LESS THAN £500K)

Project title:	Client name:
Principal contractor:	Responsible person:
Date plan prepared:	Project cost:
Project address/location:	
Person and company completing this form, if different:	
Actions taken prior to construction to reduce waste:	
Types of waste arising:	

Quantity / Material	Re-used on-site M³/T	Re-used off-site M³/T	Recycled for use on-site M³/T	Recycled for use off-site M³/T	Sent to recycling facility M³/T	Sent to WML exempt site M³/T	Disposal to landfill M³/T	Waste transfer note completed and attached?
Inert								
Non-hazardous								
Hazardous								
Totals (in M³/T)								
Performance score as %*								
SWMP target %*								

Declaration

All waste from the site will be dealt with in accordance with the Waste Duty of Care in section 34 of the Environmental Protection Act 1990 and the Environmental Protection (Duty of Care) Regulations 1991; and all materials will be handled efficiently and waste managed appropriately.

Signed: ....

For Client

Signed: ....

For Principal Contractor

Notes

WTN - Waste Transfer Note

WML - Waste Management Licence

* There is an option to use this form as a measurement tool to work out savings etc. against each waste stream.

Where applicable use additional sheets.

This data sheet must be updated whenever waste is processed or taken away from the site and expanded as necessary.

Site waste management plan
(more than £500k)

A Site Waste Management Plan (SWMP) provides a structure for waste control and disposal at all stages during a construction project.

WHAT ARE THEY FOR?

Typically, an SWMP will help to identify:

- who will be responsible for resource management on site

- what types of waste will be generated on site

- how the waste will be managed - will it be reduced, reused or recycled

- which contractors will be used to ensure the waste is correctly recycled or disposed of responsibly and legally

- how the quantity of waste generated from the project will be measured.

USEFUL TOOL

Our completed **Site Waste Management Plan (more than £500k)** will become a useful tool that shows how resources have been used and waste managed on your construction site, giving you valuable information for the future. It can help your business avoid prosecution by making sure all waste leaving site ends up in the right place. It also could help to cut costs. Remember that the information input to the SWMP will need to be developed to suit your particular project to make it work.

ADDITIONAL INFORMATION

For projects with a value of more that £500,000 additional information is needed. The second page of our document spells out what's required.

SITE WASTE MANAGEMENT PLAN (MORE THAN £500K)

Project title:	Client name:
Principal contractor:	Responsible person:
Date plan prepared:	Project cost:
Project address/location:	
Person and company completing this form, if different:	
Actions taken prior to construction to reduce waste:	
Types of waste arising:	

Quantity / Material	Re-used on-site M³/T	Re-used off-site M³/T	Recycled for use on-site M³/T	Recycled for use off-site M³/T	Sent to recycling facility M³/T	Sent to WML, exempt site M³/T	Disposal to landfill M³/T	Waste transfer note completed and attached?
Inert								
Non- hazardous								
hazardous								
Totals (in M³/T)								
Performance score as %*								
SWMP target %*								

Declaration

All waste from the site will be dealt with in accordance with the Waste Duty of Care in section 34 of the Environmental Protection Act 1990 and the Environmental Protection (Duty of Care) Regulations 1991; and all materials will be handled efficiently and waste managed appropriately.

Signed: ....

For Client

Signed: ....

For Principal Contractor

Notes

WTN - Waste Transfer Note

WML - Waste Management Licence

* There is an option to use this form as a measurement tool to work out savings etc. against each waste stream.

Where applicable use additional sheets.

This data sheet must be updated whenever waste is processed or taken away from the site and expanded as necessary.

Compliance questionnaire

The following questions must be completed within three months of the completion of the project.

Point	Review	Yes	No
1	Has the plan been reviewed?		
2	Have the types and quantities of waste produced been recorded?		
3	Has the plan been updated to reflect the progress of the project?		
4	Has a comparison of the estimated quantities of each waste type, against the actual amounts created, been completed?		
5	Have there been any significant deviations from the plan?		
6	Can you provide an estimate of the cost savings achieved by completing and implementing the plan?		

Further information:

Please provide additional information to support the answers to the above questions here:

....

....

....

....

Signed: ....

For Client

Signed: ....

For Principal Contractor

Waste minimisation and recycling policy

The only way of minimising waste effectively is if all your employees follow a formal waste minimisation and recycling policy. Adapt our document to suit your business and add it to your existing policies and procedures.

WASTE MINIMISATION AND RECYCLING

Our **Waste Minimisation and Recycling Policy** clearly identifies how you intend to manage waste within your business. It's split into two sections; the first is a general statement that spells out your commitment to managing and minimising waste. The second section includes a number of specific aims. These might not apply to all businesses; as such, you should amend these to suit.

WASTE MINIMISATION AND RECYCLING POLICY

1. General statement

It is our policy to ensure a high level of commitment to good environmental practice throughout our activities. This document expands on that policy as it relates to waste minimisation and recycling.

It is intended to develop the existing Environmental Policy by minimising the production of waste through good purchasing practice, reuse and economic recycling.

To help ensure we give proper consideration to our environmental management responsibilities, and to assist in the minimisation of waste and the recycling of materials wherever practicable, systems and procedures will be implemented to encourage the recycling and reuse of materials with a view to minimising the overall levels of waste produced by this organisation. All staff are expected to abide by the following procedures and co-operate with management in the execution of this Policy.

2. Specific aims

As part of our commitment to protecting the environment and reducing the level of waste, we have adopted the following specific aims:

- cultivate a work ethic with a high level of awareness of waste minimisation and recycling

- promote economy in the use of paper and the selection of print formats and document styles in line with this

- encourage the purchase of recycled materials and those which are suitable for disposal by recycling

- favour suppliers who operate according to sound environmental principles

- minimise waste by encouraging the exchange, and re-use of equipment and materials amongst departments

- develop a waste management strategy which accommodates recycling procedures and initiatives

- develop a wide range of recycling schemes

- encourage departments to establish local recycling schemes which are relevant to their individual activities.

3. Paper-based products

Almost any type of cardboard or paper, from daily newspapers to brown lunch paper bags, from normal office photocopier/printer paper to catalogues or from cardboard wine cases to paper potato bags can be recycled.

It is essential to avoid any synthetic materials such as plasticised papers, tinfoils, waxed papers or any other plastic or metal binders or wrappings, e.g. crisp bags, sweet/biscuit wrappers and milk/juice cartons. Such materials should go into normal waste bins.

Clearly identified cardboard bins or trays will be placed in each office for collection of all suitable waste paper.

Only paper suitable for recycling should be placed in these containers.

Cleaning staff will empty these containers on a daily basis and take the waste paper to centrally located collection points. All cleaning staff will be notified of these collection points. The central waste paper skip will be uplifted and emptied on a monthly basis.

4. Future recycling

We are committed to expanding our Recycling Policy. Procedures for recycling other wastes will be developed and implemented over time.

Other schemes which the company will investigate include:

- composting of organic and bio-degradable materials

- recovery and recycling of ferrous-based products

- collection of and recycling of glass-based products

- recycling of materials, including timber products, aggregates and excavated material.

Guidance note - selection and management of waste contractors

Although the Environment Agency, Defra and the local authorities are doing their best to remove the cowboys from the waste business, unfortunately, many still exist. To help you to avoid the dodgy ones, use our guidance note.

WASTE MANAGEMENT CONTRACTOR SELECTION AND MANAGEMENT

As with the selection of any contractor or service provider, it is essential that those used are competent, suitably experienced and have adequate resources. To aid and assist your decision process, use our **Guidance Note - Selection and Management of Waste Contractors**. It will help you select a contractor who is up to the task of removing your waste, satisfies all of the applicable legal requirements and will find a solution that works well for your business.

GUIDANCE NOTE -
SELECTION AND MANAGEMENT OF WASTE CONTRACTORS

Legal position:

Under the **Environmental Protection (Duty of Care) Regulations 1991**, all producers and handlers of waste are required to "take reasonable measures to prevent the unauthorised deposit, treatment or disposal of waste". Therefore, when you engage a waste management contractor to transport and dispose of your waste, you have a legal obligation to ensure that it is disposed of in an authorised and responsible manner. In order to comply with these Regulations, there are specific considerations that need to be taken into account.

- ensure that the contractor is registered to carry the specific class of waste or determine whether or not they are exempt. If necessary, request to see a copy of the company's registration certificate or check directly with the Environment Agency
- ensure that the contractor provides you with a waste transfer or consignment note
- ensure that the contractor disposes of the waste to a licensed landfill site, transfer station or other licensed facility (ask for documented evidence).

When selecting a potential waste management contractor, give consideration to the following factors:

- discuss your waste types and quantities. The contractor may have useful contacts, tips or advice that can help to save you money

- ensure that they fully understand the complexities and issues surrounding the generation of waste within your workplace

- request details on different waste disposal options

- enquire about different collection times and frequencies and assess the ability of the contractor to respond to your needs and the cost implications that changes to these arrangements may have

- ensure that the contractor is registered with the appropriate regulator and that details of their registration are openly displayed at their offices or that they offer to show it to you without you having to request it

- request details of any relevant professional or trade bodies that the company may belong to

- ensure established systems are in place for the generation and efficient issue of waste transfer notes and consignment notes

- confirm the regular disposal routes/locations for wastes similar to your own

- enquire if the contractor has attained ISO 14001 or ISO 9001 certification

- request details of other businesses in the area who use the contractor's services, speak to the clients and obtain feedback on the quality of service.

By selecting and working in partnership with a competent waste management contractor, the management and disposal of waste can be carried out in a much more efficient manner. Some of the issues that should be considered include:

- **Waste segregation.** Separating and segregating specific types of waste, such as paper, plastic, metal and glass, can help to reduce disposal costs and aid recycling initiatives. Consider using specific colour-coded bins for the collection and subsequent disposal/recycling of wastes.

- **Formal waste collection point.** By establishing a central on-site waste facility for all types of waste, it is more likely that staff will make the effort to segregate wastes. It also makes it easier for the contractor to handle and dispose of the waste.

- **Select appropriate waste skips.** Work with your waste management contractor to determine the most suitable type(s) and size of waste bins/skips for your site. Both oversized and undersized skips can result in unnecessary additional costs to your organisation.

- **Waste compaction.** Discuss with your contractor the options for utilising waste baling or compaction equipment. This can be particularly beneficial for companies which generate large volumes of paper, cardboard and plastic. Compacting waste reduces the number of waste collections required, cuts the amount of on-site storage required and facilitates recycling of such materials.

- **Agree costs.** As with any business contract, ensure that all costs are agreed in advance together with any mechanism for reviewing them, both up, and down! Also ensure that you understand how you are being charged. For example, is it based on the number of skips emptied or the weight of the waste contained within the skip?

- **Utilise the contractor's skills and knowledge.** Finally, as with any other professional, always ask your waste management contractor for advice on how they would deal with a particular situation. It is likely that they can bring you not only their own experience and knowledge, but also that gained from other customers.

Chapter 6

Water

Register of environmental legislation - water

Our Register of Environmental Legislation - Water helps to identify the law relating to water which applies to your business and what you're doing about it.

WHY YOU NEED OUR REGISTER

Our **Register of Environmental Legislation - Water** will show that you're up-to-date with the latest legal requirements. This can be useful if you're inspected by the Environment Agency, if clients ask environmental questions during vetting procedures, or if you want to go for certification under ISO14001.

ADAPTING THE CONTENTS

After a short introduction, the Register includes a table with four columns:

1. Legislation

2. Summary

3. Regulator

4. Aspects of activities affected.

The first three columns are pre-completed with information regarding the particular law, whilst the fourth is free for you to provide details of how the legislation affects your business.

REGISTER OF ENVIRONMENTAL LEGISLATION - WATER

Introduction

The Environmental Management Standard ISO 14001 recommends that each organisation "establishes and maintains a procedure to identify and have access to legal and other requirements to which the organisation subscribes, that are applicable to the environmental aspects of its activities, products or services."

It is the purpose of this register of environmental legislation to demonstrate compliance with this standard.

Part 2 Water

Note. This table lists the most commonly applicable legislation relating to water. *(Delete and amend as required and complete the "Impact" column as appropriate to your business.)*

Legislation	Summary	Regulator	Impact - Aspects of activities affected (Describe how and why the legislation affects you. Refer to associated internal documents)
Water Resources Act 1991 (amended by the Environment Act 1995 and the Water Resources Act 1991 (Amendment) (England and Wales) Regulations 2009)	The principal piece of legislation regarding discharges to controlled waters. The Act makes it an offence to cause or knowingly permit any poisonous, noxious or polluting matter or any solid waste matter to enter controlled waters. The 2009 amendment extended the use of Water Protection Zones and Works Notices to deal with harm to aquatic ecosystems caused by the physical characteristics of a watercourse, such as the condition of river banks	Environment Agency (EA)	*e.g. Under this legislation we have a duty to prevent pollution to nearby watercourses.*

Legislation	Summary	Regulator	Impact - Aspects of activities affected (Describe how and why the legislation affects you. Refer to associated internal documents)
Environmental Permitting (England and Wales) Regulations 2010	Provides a consolidated system for environmental permits (and exemptions) for industrial activities, mobile plant, waste operations, mining waste operations, water discharge activities, groundwater activities and radioactive substances activities. The Regulations replace the Environmental Permitting (England and Wales) Regulations 2007 (which provided a system for permitting waste operations, mining waste operations, mobile plant and installations), the system of consenting of water discharges in Chapter 2 of Part 3 of the Water Resources Act 1991 (c.57), the groundwater permitting system in the Groundwater (England and Wales) Regulations 2009 and the system of radioactive substances regulation in the Radioactive Substances Act 1993 (c.12).	EA	*e.g. We have an environmental permit for discharge to the river …(insert river). The document is held by …(insert name) and …(insert name) is responsible for ensuring compliance.*

Legislation	Summary	Regulator	Impact - Aspects of activities affected (Describe how and why the legislation affects you. Refer to associated internal documents)
Groundwater Regulations 1998	Prohibits direct or indirect discharge of certain dangerous substances to groundwater and sets out arrangements for the control of pollution resulting from the discharge of those and other substances.	EA	*e.g. We are not located in a groundwater source protection zone.*
Salmon and Freshwater Fisheries Act 1975	Under the Act it is an offence to discharge effluent into controlled waters which will result in damage to fish, their food, spawn or spawning grounds.	EA	*e.g. We are located close to the ...(insert river) river and ensure that we comply with our environmental permit conditions in relation to our discharges.*
Anti-Pollution Works Regulations 1999	These regulations enable the EA to serve a notice on a polluter or potential polluter to remedy or prevent water pollution. The Regulations set out the contents of anti-pollution works notices, how to appeal against such notices, and how to claim compensation for access rights in connection with anti-pollution works.	EA	

Legislation	Summary	Regulator	Impact - Aspects of activities affected (Describe how and why the legislation affects you. Refer to associated internal documents)
Water Act 2003	The Act sets procedures relating to applications for abstraction licences, regulates impoundments and includes measures for drought management and flood defence work in England and Wales.	EA	*e.g. We are not affected by this legislation as we do not abstract water from boreholes or watercourses.*
Control of Pollution (Oil Storage) (England) Regulations 2001 *(check equivalent national legislation for requirements as applicable)*	These regulations impose general requirements for preventing pollution of controlled waters from oil storage, particularly fixed tanks or mobile bowsers. The regulations require that where more than 200 litres of oil is stored above ground on non-domestic premises, tanks must be of robust construction and bunded to 110% capacity.	EA	

Legislation	Summary	Regulator	Impact - Aspects of activities affected (Describe how and why the legislation affects you. Refer to associated internal documents)
Environmental Damage (Prevention and Remediation) Regulations 2009 (These apply to England - check equivalent national legislation for requirements as applicable)	The regulations require that environmental damage is made good and that where there is a risk of environmental damage, action is taken to prevent it. Where damage has occurred, there is a duty to inform the EA and take advice on what must be carried out in terms of repair. Where the EA has to undertake the repair on behalf of an organisation, the costs can be recharged.	EA, Natural England, Councils	
Nitrate Pollution Prevention Regulations 2008 (as amended)	Controls the amount of nitrogen fertiliser and organic manure spread on agricultural land.	EA	*e.g. We are not affected by this legislation.*
Trade Effluent (Prescribed Processes and Substances) Regulations 1989 (as amended 1990)	Specifies which categories of trade effluent have their discharge to public sewers controlled. Also requires sewerage undertakers to notify Environment Agency if they intend to vary existing trade effluent consents.	EA/water companies	

Legislation	Summary	Regulator	Impact - Aspects of activities affected (Describe how and why the legislation affects you. Refer to associated internal documents)
Water Resources (Environmental Impact Assessment) (England and Wales) Regulations 2003	Requires an assessment of the likely environmental impact of projects abstracting over 20 cubic metres of water in 24 hours and agricultural water management projects, including irrigation projects.	EA	

Water efficiency policy and procedure

Many people seem to believe there is an endless supply of fresh clean water. However, a growing population and increasing levels of pollution are threatening the availability of water. Water restrictions are likely to become more common in the future and the price of water, which has already increased significantly over the last ten years, is set to rise further. Therefore, there has never been a greater incentive to manage and reduce the amount of water used within the workplace.

WATER EFFICIENCY

Reductions and efficiencies can be achieved through the adoption of a number of relatively simple, yet effective, techniques. These will not only demonstrate your organisation's commitment to the environment, but also have significant cost benefits. Our **Water Efficiency Policy and Procedure** will provide you with the basis for implementing such changes within your own workplace.

WATER EFFICIENCY
POLICY AND PROCEDURE

1. General statement

It is our policy to ensure that wastage and inefficient use of water resources within the workplace is kept to an acceptable level.

As a business customer, we pay for all the water that passes through our meter so it makes sound financial sense to ensure we are not pouring money down the drain. We also recognise that water is a precious resource, and that the way we use it has implications for the environment, both through the demand we place on local water resources, and through our potential to pollute the water we use.

To help ensure we give due and proper consideration to our environmental management responsibilities, and to assist in the minimisation of water consumption and the efficient use of water in the workplace, this Policy and Procedure will be implemented to prevent unnecessary wastage. All staff are expected to abide by this Procedure and co-operate with management in the execution of this Policy.

2. Legal position

The main legislation governing the efficient use of water and the minimisation of wastage is found in sections 71-75 of the **Water Industry Act 1991**.

Under the Act, it is an offence, either through negligence or intentionally, to allow water fittings to remain in disrepair so as to cause the contamination, wasting or misuse of water. Water authorities are empowered to enter any premises to check the installation of any water fittings and for compliance with these requirements.

3. Management of water use

Further to the general statement above, we aim to reflect our commitment to sustainable development through the way we use water in our organisation.

Accordingly we will:

- use water efficiently
- avoid causing water pollution
- minimise expenditure on water consumption.

In order to achieve this we will:

- monitor the consumption of water within our buildings and premises

- identify buildings/processes with high water consumption

- introduce cost-effective water-saving devices where appropriate

- promptly repair leaks where identified on the Company's premises

- work in partnership with water companies and the Environment Agency to help conserve water and reduce pollution

- raise awareness about the environmental implications of water use and promote good housekeeping practice.

4. Procedures

The first step is to establish the amount of water used. This can be done by looking at historic water bills to see if there have been any significant increases in usage (this may, however, be due to increases in staff numbers or new work processes). The installation of a water meter will enable the exact volumes of water used to be more closely monitored (if not already installed).

Find and fix leaks

- where a water meter is fitted, check for leaks by turning off the main stop tap, and taking two meter readings several minutes apart. If the reading is different, there may be a leak

- leaks are more likely to occur in the supply pipes located below or adjacent to your premises

- contact your supplier if you are unsure where the source of increased water use is. Some water authorities provide free water audits

- check for leaks in toilet cisterns, overflows and pipe-work for the heating and hot/cold water supplies around the building

- check all areas where water is used in your office/building. A dripping tap can waste as much as 90 litres a week.

Simple water saving techniques

- install a special water saving devices in toilet cisterns, such as the inexpensive "Save a flush" and "Hog Bag". Some water authorities will provide these free of charge to their customers, however they do not work with all toilet types.

New fittings

- fit spray inserts in regularly-used taps. These reduce the amount of water discharged through the tap but do not reduce washing efficiency

- fit new percussion taps, which turn off after a set period

- fit variable flush handles to all applicable toilet cisterns. Standard toilets use between six and nine litres of water every time they are flushed

- if replacing automatic flushing urinals, consider proximity flush control systems, or use waterless and air flush systems where possible. Fit supply restrictor valves in supply pipes. These maintain a steady water flow, whatever the change in water pressure and can reduce water flow by up to 50%

- where washing machines and dishwashers are used, make sure they are the most water and energy-efficient.

Consider collecting rainwater for alternative uses

- rainwater can be collected in water butts and used for various processes such as watering gardens, washing vehicles and general cleaning.

Efficient water use within the office

- ensure that everyone is aware of the need to be water-efficient

- do not over-fill kettles, use only enough water for your needs at any particular time. This has the added benefit of also reducing your energy bills

- water can be saved by turning the hot tap down, rather than the cold tap up, if cooler water is required

- use a plug in the sink and a bowl of water to wash cups and plates rather than washing under the tap over an open plughole.

Water pollution risks checklist

Water pollution can occur by accidental run-off, process failures which exceed permitted discharge levels, and incorrect management of plant or storage areas etc. To help you assess and manage the risks we've produced a Water Pollution Risks Checklist.

CONSIDERATIONS

The first half of our checklist asks whether you've considered the risk arising from various common water pollution hazards. There are twelve in total including oil/fuel storage, litter, fire fighting and vehicle washing. As well as identifying whether each risk has been considered, there's a check that you've done something about it, i.e. controlled the risk. Each question on our checklist can be answered "Yes", "No", or "N/A".

TEST OF KNOWLEDGE

The second part of the checklist runs through various pieces of information which you should have in your possession. These enable you to decide upon the correct risk control measures and influence your actions in an emergency. The questions cover information about the local environment, drains on site, discharge consents and previous enforcement action.

WATER POLLUTION RISKS CHECKLIST

Have you considered the risk, as applicable, from:	Y	N	N/A
Oil/fuel storage and dispensing areas?	❏	❏	❏
Run-off from roads and roofs?	❏	❏	❏
Construction works due to take place near neighbouring watercourses?	❏	❏	❏
Forseeable emergencies including fire fighting run-off?	❏	❏	❏
Wastes arising from processes on site, e.g. manufacturing?	❏	❏	❏
Storage of waste and raw materials?	❏	❏	❏
Discharge of fire extinguishers (except plain water and carbon dioxide) during servicing or training exercises?	❏	❏	❏
Accidental spillages?	❏	❏	❏
Site litter which may blow into watercourses?	❏	❏	❏
Vehicle washing?	❏	❏	❏
Sewage plant failure (if you have your own plant)?	❏	❏	❏
Septic tanks?	❏	❏	❏
Are you confident that you have implemented risk control measures for all of these hazards and any others that apply?	❏	❏	❏

Do you know:

	Y	N	N/A
If there are restrictions which apply because of local environmental sensitivity, e.g. groundwater protection zone?	❏	❏	❏
What restrictions apply to your trade effluent discharges?	❏	❏	❏
- and are you sure that you are well within the limits on quantity, rate of discharge and composition?	❏	❏	❏
Which drains on site are foul and which are surface water?	❏	❏	❏
- and are these clearly marked?	❏	❏	❏
Where surface water drains lead, e.g. local stream, soakaway, pond?	❏	❏	❏
Where oil separators are installed (where applicable)?	❏	❏	❏

	Y	N	N/A

That there are no concerns about connections to the surface
water drainage system, i.e. illegal wastewater connections? ❏ ❏ ❏

What conditions apply to water discharges under Environment
Agency Consents/ Permits, if applicable? ❏ ❏ ❏

That no previous enforcement action has been taken or
considered in relation to water pollution incidents? ❏ ❏ ❏

- if the answer is "No", i.e. there has been previous
  enforcement action taken or considered, have reliable
  measures been implemented to prevent a recurrence of
  the problem? ❏ ❏ ❏

Comments/further action to be taken:

....

....

....

This checklist has been completed to the best of my knowledge.

Signed .... Date ....

Note. This checklist is to be retained on file for at least three years.

Guidance note - grey water recycling and rainwater harvesting

Techniques such as rainwater harvesting and grey water recycling can provide financially viable methods to significantly reduce the amount of water used within the workplace.

REDUCTION OF WATER USED

In addition to reducing the volume of expensive mains water used, rainwater harvesting and grey water recycling have the advantage of reducing the volume of waste water and storm water that would otherwise be disposed of to the sewerage system. Our **Guidance Note - Grey Water Recycling and Rainwater Harvesting** provides more information on how they work.

GUIDANCE NOTE -
GREY WATER RECYCLING AND RAINWATER HARVESTING

Grey water recycling

The term "grey water" is used to define the waste water produced from baths, showers, washing machines, and wash-hand basins. It does not include the wastewater from toilets, kitchen sinks or dishwashers which is called black water due to its higher organic content. As the name suggests, grey water is of lesser quality than drinking water, but of higher quality than black water.

Using grey water can save up to 18,000 litres of water a year within an average domestic property. This represents approximately one-third of the water typically used, and is equivalent to all the water required for toilet flushing. Grey water can be used for things like toilet flushing, car washing and garden irrigation, however it does require some treatment before being used. This usually consists of basic disinfecting or microbiological treatment. However, problems can arise when the warm, nutrient-rich grey water is stored for any length of time, since it quickly deteriorates as bacteria multiply.

To help improve the quality and life of grey water it is a matter of best practice to filter it prior to disinfection. This has the advantage of removing gross matter such as hair and skin debris on which most of the bacterial activity will be centred. The use of filtering combined with disinfection prevents biological activity for long enough to allow any treated grey water to be stored until it is needed.

The basic components of a grey water recycling system are:

- separate drainage collection system to avoid cross contamination with black water

- suitably sized storage tank

- filter for screening water

- disinfectant dosing system

- pump to remove water from the storage tank into a header tank feeding the toilet

- header tank.

To provide a safeguard against running dry, a mains-fed water supply should also be available for the toilets. Finally, the system must also incorporate a means of protecting the mains water supply against contamination by backflow (in order to comply with the **Water Supply (Water Fittings) Regulations 1999**). All pipework containing treated grey water should also be clearly marked to avoid it accidentally being mistaken for mains water.

For larger commercial installations grey water can be treated in the same way as sewage. This can be achieved using traditional biological treatment systems, though these tend to be expensive to operate and maintain. Alternatively a more practical solution is to use a membrane treatment facility which provides a very high level of filtration. When using these forms of grey water treatment, it is possible, depending on the type of process used, to treat the combined sewage flow without the need to separate out the grey and black waters. The treated water from these systems is clear and free of unpleasant odour and contains little organic matter, allowing it to be stored and used for much longer periods of time. The low level of contamination following this type of treatment means that far lower levels of disinfection need to be used.

At the most basic level, untreated grey water can be used for garden watering providing it is used soon after it has been produced/collected.

Rainwater harvesting

Rainwater harvesting simply involves the collection of rainwater that would otherwise have been collected and discharged into the sewerage system, lost into the ground or which would have evaporated into the atmosphere. Large impermeable surfaces such as roofs, car parks, hard standings or driveways are ideal for rainwater harvesting and can provide significant quantities of water from even small areas. The water collected can be used to flush the toilet, water gardens and even supply the washing machine. Rainwater harvesting systems can be installed in most types of property, both domestic and commercial/industrial and in both new and existing buildings. The water used is generally of a much higher quality than grey water and can be used for most purposes other than as drinking water.

However if roads, driveways and other hard standings on which vehicles operate are to be incorporated into a rainwater harvesting system, care needs to be taken to avoid possible contamination from oil leaks and spilt petrol/diesel etc. The use of petrol interceptors in such instances can help to reduce the risk of such contamination, though the use of rainwater collected just from roof areas will provide higher quality water.

For many existing businesses and new developments there can be clear financial benefits to installing a rainwater harvesting system. The savings that can be achieved against the metered costs of mains water can be substantial, enabling the installation costs of the system to be recovered relatively quickly. If, however, water is only required for irrigation or garden watering, then a much cheaper and simpler option is to simply install a series of water butts.

A number of different rainwater harvesting systems are available from specialist suppliers, however most systems work on the basis of collecting rainwater from roofed areas which is transported via normal guttering and down pipes to an underground storage tank. Leaves and debris are generally filtered out prior to it entering the tank.

The water within the storage tank will be monitored. If the water level falls below a pre-determined point, the tank will be topped up from the mains water supply and if it gets too high, the contents will overflow out of the tank to a surface water drain. As the water is not suitable for drinking, its use will be limited to flushing toilets, supplying garden taps and washing machines. As with a grey water system, separate supply pipe work will be required to avoid any cross-contamination with the mains water.

The reduction in water usage has both environmental and financial benefits, though the extent of any financial benefits will be dependent on the annual levels of rainfall in the area, the demand for the water, maintenance needs and the lifetime of the parts before they need replacing. Larger projects such as housing developments, industrial premises and agricultural irrigation schemes will have relatively short payback times and savings could run into many thousands of pounds.

However, before committing to a rainwater harvesting system, make sure an evaluation of the volume of rainfall that can be collected from the relevant impermeable areas has been carried out and that an economically viable solution exists.

Other advantages of water reuse

The reduction in sewage volume is another important advantage of grey water and rainfall harvesting systems, especially for developments with private drainage and treatment systems. For individuals and organisations who pay for mains drainage, a reduction in sewerage charges may be negotiable with the relevant sewerage authority.

Waste water management policy
and procedure

The increasing use of chemicals and pollutants, coupled with the rapid urbanisation of large parts of the country, means that the pollution and contamination of our natural water resources is occurring on a more regular and significant basis.

WASTE WATER MANAGEMENT POLICY AND PROCEDURES

To counter the rise in this kind of incident, a policy of "the polluter pays" is in force. Those responsible for causing pollution can be made to pay the total clean-up costs of any pollution incident that they are found to be responsible for. Our **Waste Water Management Policy and Procedure** can be adopted and implemented to help manage and control discharges of waste water from your premises, thereby helping to minimise any impact on the environment, and prevent a costly clean-up operation.

WASTE WATER MANAGEMENT
POLICY AND PROCEDURE

1. General statement

It is our policy to ensure that waste water discharges from our undertakings are properly managed and controlled, whilst at all times minimising the impact of such discharges on the natural environment.

As a business customer, we are required to pay for the collection, transport and treatment of any waste water that is discharged from our premises into the public sewerage system. We also recognise that water is a precious resource, and that the way we use and dispose of it has implications for the environment.

To help ensure we give proper consideration to our environmental management responsibilities, and to assist in the management and control of waste water discharges, this Policy and Procedure will be implemented to demonstrate how our organisation manages its responsibilities. All staff are expected to abide by this Procedure and co-operate with management in the execution of this Policy.

2. Legal position

The main legislation governing the control, management and treatment of waste water is:

- the **Urban Waste Water Treatment (England and Wales) Regulations 1994**

- and the **Water Act 2003**.

The **Urban Waste Water Treatment Regulations** specify the criteria and requirement for the treatment and discharge of waste water into rivers, estuaries and coastal waters. They also identify sensitive and less sensitive waters and introduced measures to ban the dumping of sludge at sea.

The **Water Act**, in conjunction with the **Water Industry Act**, requires an application to be submitted and authorised by the relevant sewerage authority before any discharge of waste water or trade effluent is made into the public sewerage system. The application is required to detail the composition, volume and frequency of discharges, as well as any measures that have been taken to minimise the impact of the discharge on sewerage services.

3. Procedures and arrangements for the management of waste water

Further to the general statement above, we aim to reflect our commitment to managing our waste water discharges by carefully monitoring and controlling our activities so that the risks associated with pollution and waste water discharges are proactively managed.

Accordingly, we will:

- avoid causing pollution as far as is reasonably practicable

- minimise the volume of waste water generated by our activities.

In order to achieve this we will:

- monitor the consumption of water within our buildings and premises

- identify buildings with high water consumption

- introduce cost-effective water-saving devices where appropriate

- repair leaks where identified on the company's premises

- use drip trays/catch pots on plant and equipment which has the potential to leak oil, fuel or other chemicals

- ensure that all potential pollutants are stored safely and securely within appropriately bunded areas

- all contaminated water and other liquids with any bund, drip tray or catch pot will be collected and disposed of off site by an appropriately licensed waste contractor and not disposed off down the drain

- drainage from all large hard-standing areas where vehicular movements may occur will be drained via an oil/petrol interceptor before being discharged into the public sewerage system

- waste oil storage tanks and oil/petrol interceptors will be fitted with high level alarms that provide an audible/visual alarm when the tank is nearing its full capacity, this will act as a prompt to ensure that the tank is emptied as necessary

- re-fuelling of vehicles, plant and machinery will, where appropriate, be carried out in areas where the risk of pollution from a spill is minimal and where any spills can be easily contained and cleaned up

- it will not be permitted to allow spills to simply be washed down or swept into the nearest drain. A sufficient supply of emergency spill kits and emergency drain covers will therefore be available in order to contain and clean up any spilt material

- staff will not be permitted to empty any waste chemicals, oils or cleaning products down any drain, sewer, toilet or sink

- care will be taken when ordering and during deliveries to ensure that fuel, and other chemicals are not over-ordered, leading to the overfilling of tanks and spills to the surrounding areas

- delivery hoses are to be fully drained into their corresponding storage tank to ensure that excess material is not deposited on the ground or within the drains serving that area

- all staff will receive appropriate training and instruction on the company's policy and procedures and what action should be taken in the event of a potential pollution causing incident.

Guidance note - discharge consent

In some instances, it's necessary to discharge effluent or waste water into a local watercourse or tidal water. In such circumstances, organisations are required to obtain permission from the regulatory authorities, such as the Environment Agency.

DISCHARGE CONSENTS

Under the **Water Resources Act 1991**, any business that discharges a substance that has the potential to cause harm to the environment must obtain the consent of the Environment Agency. However, this is not a simple task. And, if the consent is granted, you will need to know how to comply with it. To help you through this complex process, use our **Guidance Note - Discharge Consent** document. It covers all the points you'll need to know before, during and even after you gain consent for your discharge.

GUIDANCE NOTE - DISCHARGE CONSENT

Introduction

Any person or organisation who discharges rainwater, cooling water, sewage, waste water or treated liquid effluents directly into controlled waters is likely to require a discharge consent.

In England and Wales, the Environment Agency (EA) is responsible for granting discharge consents. In Scotland it's the Scottish Environment Protection Agency (SEPA).

Discharge consents are generally either:

Numeric. These consents are used where the discharges have the greatest potential to impact on the quality of the receiving water. The consent specifies numerical concentration limits that apply to an individual substance or group of substances contained in the discharge.

Descriptive. These are used where the discharges are small, with a low potential risk to the environment, and where it would otherwise be difficult to control the discharge by means of specific numerical values. The consents define the nature of the treatment process, together with a requirement that the plant is correctly operated and maintained.

In circumstances where it is feasible for property to connect directly to a public sewer, the EA will not normally consider granting a discharge consent.

Background

If you or your company discharges rainwater, cooling water, sewage, waste water or treated liquid effluents directly into controlled waters, you are required to obtain the consent of the EA or SEPA/the Environment and Heritage Service as appropriate.

It is an offence to cause pollution of controlled waters and any responsible organisation will be conscious of the potential impact and consequences its discharges may have on the receiving water. In these cases procedures and controls to restrict and minimise the effect of such discharges must be implemented.

The EA levy both application and annual fees for each discharge consent, the costs of which are dependent, amongst other things, on the volume and pollutant load contained within the discharge.

What are controlled waters?

Controlled waters include:

- surface watercourses such as open ditches, streams and rivers, ponds, lakes and lochs

- groundwater contained in underground strata, or in wells or boreholes

- tidal estuaries

- coastal waters.

Which discharges need a consent?

Surface water discharges from industrial and commercial premises are designed to carry clean, uncontaminated rainwater. Where a risk of contamination in the form of either sewage or other contaminant such as fuel, oil, chemicals or other pollutants exists, the discharges should be made to an appropriate sewer. Where this is not applicable, the EA should be approached to discuss obtaining a discharge consent.

Generally, discharges of the following types will require a discharge consent. If a discharge consent is not applicable, the EA will advise accordingly:

- drainage from roofs and hardstandings in many industries

- drainage from garage forecourts and fuel delivery/storage areas

- drainage from raw material delivery areas

- drainage from material storage areas

- direct discharges of treated wastewater from treatment plants

- water from external washing and cleaning activities

- sewage or septic tank drainage from industrial or commercial premises.

Legislation applying to discharges to controlled waters

England and Wales **Water Resources Act 1991** (as amended).

Scotland Control of **Pollution Act 1974** (as amended).

Northern Ireland **Water (Northern Ireland) Order 1999**.

Offences

It is an offence to cause pollution of controlled water, deliberately or accidentally. It is an offence to breach a discharge consent condition and an Enforcement Notice can be served on the holder of the consent. Failure to comply with an Enforcement Notice can result in a fine of up to £20,000 or imprisonment of up to two years.

How do you apply, and what are the application fees?

Contact the EA to discuss your requirements and to obtain an application form.

- a separate application and fee is required for each different effluent that is to be discharged

- a reduced application fee may apply where the proposed discharge is less than $5m^3/$ day of sewage, or less than $10m^3$ of trade effluent from cooling or heat exchange equipment, or is surface water without any trade effluent.

Annual charges for discharge consents

The annual charge is based on:

- the volume factor relating to the maximum permitted discharge per day

- the content factor relating to the amount and nature of the pollutants discharged

- the receiving water factor relating to the type/class of receiving water

- the financial factor relating to the particular year.

The following information represents the type of information that is required to be included on each discharge consent application form.

Details of the discharge

- the maximum discharge quantities in cubic metres per day

- co-ordinates of each discharge point

- details of where the discharges may be sampled for compliance monitoring purposes

- the volume of effluent discharged may in some cases need to be monitored. Facilities to enable the EA to measure the volume must be provided. In some cases there will be a requirement to monitor the volume on a regular basis and maintain a log of the readings. Details of the siting and type of flow measurement facilities should be provided

- details should be given of all existing discharge consents.

Details of receiving environment

- for discharges to coastal waters, details of the length of the outfall, distance below low water and dispersion characteristics should be supplied

- where a foul sewer is available, consent may not be granted unless sufficient evidence is provided to prove connection to the foul sewer is impracticable

- the applicant should attach a site plan (preferably A4 size) showing in detail:

  - the location of the premises. For rainfall dependent discharges, the contributing catchment areas should be highlighted

  - the discharge, sampling points and any other information requested in the application form clearly marked with arrows and labels as necessary

- details of the application may need to be published in accordance with the **Water Resources Act 1991** (as amended by the **Environment Act 1995**.) In such cases, the application will be advertised in a local newspaper and in the London Gazette by the EA. The EA may request the costs associated with this advertising, together with an administration charge from the applicant.

Details of application and other information

- status of the applicant, (i.e. limited company, partnership, trader, individuals)

- if the application is by:

  - a company, then the registered office address and the company registration number should be given in addition to the full company name

  - a firm or partnership, then the full names and addresses of all the relevant partners should be given together with the name the firm trades under and its main addresses

  - a club, then the full names and addresses of all trustees should be given or the name and address of the person properly authorised to be the consent holder on behalf of the club, in the absence of any trustees

  - a charity, which is a limited company should supply the same details listed above for "company"; alternatively if the charity is not a limited corporation, the full names and addresses of all trustees should be given

- it is an offence for any person to make a statement which they know to be false or misleading

- all application charges are payable by the applicant at the time of submission. A further annual charge may also be payable from the date of coming in to force of any consent issued

- the EA maintains a statutory register, which is available for public inspection, including details of:

  - applications for consent

  - any consent granted and conditions imposed

  - samples of effluent taken by the Agency

  - information produced by analyses of the samples and the steps taken in consequence of the information.

Chapter 7

Transport

Corporate transport policy

Reducing the amount of travelling staff are asked to do has been singled out as one good way to cut the amount of carbon a business is responsible for. And, with almost constant price rises at the petrol pump, minimising miles will save money to boot.

CUT THE CARBON

To help manage and restrict the costs associated with travel, and to reduce the environmental impact of both commuter and business-related travel, we've produced a **Corporate Transport Policy**. This can be used as it is, or modified to suit your business. It consists of a series of practical measures tailored to meet the circumstances of individual organisations. Introducing a policy such as this gives a clear indication that you're taking positive steps to reduce the amount of carbon produced by your business. And it should reduce your fuel bills through a reduction in unnecessary journeys.

CORPORATE TRANSPORT POLICY

1. General statement

The use of vehicles can negatively impact on the environment in many ways - they can cause air pollution, contribute to acid rain and global warming, and lead to the more rapid depletion of our limited reserves of fossil fuels. In recognition of this, it is our policy to ensure that, wherever reasonably practicable, we will work to reduce the environmental impact of our travel, particularly the large number of single person journeys undertaken by our employees.

Our corporate objective is therefore to reduce the pollution caused by our use of vehicles for work-related travel and to reduce the annual average work-related mileage per employee.

To help ensure we give proper consideration to our environmental management responsibilities, and to reduce the number of unnecessary business miles travelled by our employees, this Policy will be implemented, monitored and enforced throughout the workplace. All staff are expected to work towards the aims of this Policy and co-operate with management in the execution of it.

2. Policy implementation

In order to achieve our desired aims, the Policy will be implemented and achieved by:

- reducing annual mileage travelled by our employees during their working day

- reducing the number of miles travelled annually per employee, in order to get to and from work

- actively encouraging and supporting alternative modes of transport

- discouraging single person car journeys

- implementing car sharing schemes

- increasing the use of less polluting technologies and fuels.

We also recognise the positive health effects of taking more exercise and will encourage more walking and cycling. We have set the following objectives for the next five years, based on current levels:

- decrease the company's annual business mileage for cars by 5% per employee

- decrease the number of miles travelled by employees getting to and from work in a car on their own, by 10%

- reduce the amount of carbon dioxide produced through business travel and travel to/from work by 20% per employee

- regularly achieving more than 25% of employees using an alternative to car travel for getting to and from work at least once a week.

In order to evaluate the effects of this policy, we will regularly monitor and report on:

- the number of business car miles per employee per annum

- the annual amount of carbon dioxide (CO_2) generated as a result of using vehicles for work-related travel

- the percentage of people using an alternative method of transport to single person car use at least once a week.

Procedures for reducing
unnecessary journeys

Do you really need to make that journey? Often the answer is "no", but we don't think about it until it's too late. To help avoid time wasting and potentially expensive and environmentally damaging journeys, you should look at alternatives to face-to-face meetings.

REDUCING UNNECESSARY JOURNEYS

In addition to the development and implementation of a corporate policy, you might want to consider what practical steps you can take to reduce unnecessary journeys and limit the number of miles travelled by your employees. To help, why not follow our **Procedures for Reducing Unnecessary Journeys**?

PROCEDURES FOR REDUCING UNNECESSARY JOURNEYS

As part of our Corporate Transport Policy aimed at reducing the environmental impact of work-related travel, employees should be encouraged to use car and air travel more wisely. The provision of incentives to encourage employees to use alternative modes of transport and communication should also be given consideration.

The procedures for reducing unnecessary journeys can include a range of measures and techniques to address the needs of the business. The issues that need to be considered include:

- commuter journeys

- customer and visitor journeys to the office

- work-related travel

- management and purchase of company vehicles.

Benefits

The key benefits to be derived from the introduction of the Corporate Transport Policy include:

- making local communities less congested, safer and more accessible

- reducing local pollution levels of carbon dioxide, hydrocarbons, nitrogen monoxide, ozone and particulates

- reducing greenhouse gas emissions

- enabling deliveries and essential journeys to move more freely within the community, as a result of the overall reduction in the number of vehicles on the roads

- providing equal opportunities through travel incentives to everyone in the organisation, and supporting those employees without access to a car

- offering wider travel choices to staff

- providing long-term financial savings through reduced business travel costs and expenses

- helping employees to become healthier, fitter and more productive - 30 minutes a day of moderate exercise, such as cycling or brisk walking, can not only strengthen the heart and lungs, but can also help protect against ill-health

- improving the environmental image and standing of the organisation.

Promoting alternatives

Public transport

- prepare a public transport information pack with the fares and times of travel to and from work and regular business locations

- make a policy to use public transport where practicable for business purposes

- be understanding of people arriving late because of public transport delays

- provide a taxi for employees who would normally use the bus/train on occasions when they are required to work late

- provide salary advances and incentives for employees to purchase season tickets.

Bicycles

- provide free cycle helmets

- provide free high-visibility clothing

- set up an equipment pool of lights, reflective clothing and other accessories

- make battery or light chargers available in the office to charge up batteries during the day

- put up a cycling information board with cycle routes, bike repairers etc.

- provide incentive schemes, such as salary advances or company contributions to purchase bikes

- buy an office bike (or bikes) and link up with a local bike store for regular maintenance

- install shower and changing facilities during any office refurbishment works

- provide a mileage allowance for cyclists

- provide a secure place at work to store bikes and clothing during the working day.

On foot

- promote the benefits of walking to work for those who travel short distances by car. Without targeting specific people, it may be possible for some to walk to work or meetings. Provide posters and leaflets from relevant organisations.

The car

- if cars are used for regular essential journeys, promote good driving techniques. Simple techniques can help to reduce fuel consumption by as much as 25%

- ensure regular maintenance of vehicles to help maintain fuel efficiency and vehicle longevity

- if you intend to purchase a new vehicle, buy smaller more fuel-efficient models or consider purchasing a car powered by an alternative green fuel

- consider pooling car use with other organisations or joining a local car club

- consider converting existing vehicles to use Liquid Petroleum Gas (LPG)

- set up a car-share scheme within your workplace and consider extending it to other companies within your area.

Couriers

- consider using cycle couriers for delivering small items within the local area

- for longer journeys source a courier that uses gas-powered vehicles.

Deliveries/haulage

- when preparing consignments, give consideration to the volume, weight and size of the load, establish if it can be combined with other deliveries in a given area

- select a suitably sized vehicle; do not use a 38-tonne lorry for a load that can be taken in a seven-tonne lorry

- try to utilise all available space and do not take part-loads unless absolutely necessary

- with construction work, select the most economically sized lorries for haulage purposes, it may be possible to reduce the number of trips from a site by up to 50% by using lorries with a greater capacity for large earthworks projects.

Audio and video conferencing

- consider using web/phone based teleconferencing facilities for meetings where it is not essential for you to physically be at the site of a meeting. The savings generated by utilising such technologies are not only environmental, but also financial in terms of the costs saved from travelling. The initial capital expenditure of such systems can produce significant long-term financial savings.

Homeworking/tele-working

- consider implementing homeworking for staff, either on a regular or occasional basis. If work can be completed without the need to visit the office, this will not only reduce the environmental impact of work-related travel, but may also have other benefits in terms of employees' morale, health and efficiency, etc.

- if each employee spends one day a week working from home, this will reduce the environmental impact of their weekly commute by up to 20%.

Keys to success

There are several keys to the successful development and implementation of the Corporate Transport Policy.

These include:

- the implementation of the Corporate Transport Policy will involve making hard decisions and changing the habits and working practises of many members of staff. To help achieve full staff co-operation and acceptance, it is essential for senior management to positively promote the wider objectives and benefits of the Policy, and to lead by example

- it will be necessary to obtain broad support for the introduction and implementation of the Corporate Transport Policy from staff. It is essential that concerns are listened to and that any proposals are drawn up in a way that address any concerns as far as is reasonably practicable.

Time must be allowed for staff to get used to changes in travel patterns. Try not to implement everything at once.

Guidance note - alternative fuels

How much? A question we all ask ourselves each time we fill a vehicle with fuel. But are there any alternatives that will save both money and cut the amount of carbon the vehicle creates? There are, but you should make yourself aware of all the options before making a potentially expensive mistake.

ALTERNATIVE FUELS

To help you make an informed decision, we've included a **Guidance Note - Alternative Fuels**, which looks at a number of alternative fuels that are currently, or will be, available to power vehicles. The use of such fuels can have many environmental benefits, as well as offering financial savings.

GUIDANCE NOTE -
ALTERNATIVE FUELS

Traditional fuels such as petrol and diesel are generally considered as being expensive and polluting to the environment. Therefore, in response to ever increasing environmental pressures, a range of alternative fuels is now becoming available. In fact, if you use a non-petrol car, these fuels are generally cheaper and you may also qualify for further discounts and exemptions. For example, some energy-efficient cars are exempt from the London Congestion Charge. However, the biggest problem associated with alternative fuels is that they are not available everywhere.

LPG or Autogas

LPG stands for Liquefied Petroleum Gas. It is also known under several commercial names, such as Autogas. LPG occurs naturally in crude oil and natural gas production fields and it is also produced during the oil refining process. It can be easily liquefied for storage meaning it can be transported as a liquid, but burned like a gas. LPG burns more cleanly than petrol as it does not contain many of the toxic chemicals.

LPG cars are now commercially available and there is an increasing number of companies who can convert many existing petrol cars to run on LPG. It is now available at most larger filling stations throughout the country.

Hydrogen

Hydrogen is one of the most promising of all the alternative fuels, and although it is not widely available today, it is likely to be one of the main power sources for cars in the future. Hydrogen is easily produced through electrolysis. Electrolysis involves splitting water into oxygen and hydrogen, using electricity. When hydrogen is burned, it is converted into heat and water vapour, making it one of the cleanest burning fuels. Although hydrogen-powered vehicles are not commercially available, a number of car manufacturers are working on the development of cost-effective solutions.

Electricity

Electric powered cars are becoming the most popular alternative-fuel vehicles. However, although the car itself may have zero-emissions, electric powered cars do utilise power produced from conventional power stations, including fossil fuel power stations, which can be responsible for the production of large quantities of pollution.

Most of the current electric vehicles are hybrids that contain a fuel cell that uses another form of energy such as petrol. Most hybrids that are available use a combination of petrol and electric power to drive them. Hybrid cars get more miles per gallon and produce less pollution than conventional petrol-only cars. Also if one type of fuel runs out, you have a second source to keep you going.

Alcohol

Methanol and ethanol are alcohols. Ethanol is usually made from corn or biomass (agricultural biological waste). Methanol can be made from biomass like wood or coal. However, most methanol is made from natural gas, because it is cheaper. Alcohol fuels contain more power, but less energy, per gallon than petrol. This means that by using an alcohol-based fuel, your car will go faster, but you'll get fewer miles per gallon from it.

Bio-diesel

Bio-diesel is similar to normal diesel fuel, except that it is made from plant and animal waste or fat. It's not necessarily a clean burning fuel, but it is made from a renewable resource. In Australia, it's becoming a popular alternative to petrol. Bio-diesel can be used in most diesel-engine cars.

Get professional advice

If you're considering using any of the alternative fuels mentioned above, we recommend that you seek professional advice to ensure that the desired fuel is available in the areas you require it, that it is suitable for your vehicles and that it is technically/economically viable.

Chapter 8

Energy management

Energy management policy

The cost of energy used to be something that businesses didn't really pay much attention to; however, now prices have gone through the roof. To help you cut costs and to minimise your impact on the environment, follow our formal energy management policy.

RECOGNITION OF RESPONSIBLE ENERGY USE

To help you manage and control energy use in your business and to show a statement of intent to your staff and/or customers, we've created an **Energy Management Policy**. This can be included in your environmental management system and be used to show that you've recognised the importance of responsible energy use and the benefits of reducing your usage wherever practicable. You can use our policy or adapt it to fit your business, but whatever you do it should reflect the intentions of your organisation.

ENERGY MANAGEMENT POLICY

1. General statement

.........(*insert company name*) acknowledges the importance of energy as a necessary resource for successfully meeting the organisation's operational objectives. The company is committed to responsible energy management and will practice energy efficiency throughout all of its premises, utilising its plant and equipment in the most cost-effective manner to achieve this goal.

In addressing this statement, the Company will:

- incorporate energy efficiency measures, including alternative and emerging technologies, into all new and refurbished facilities through best practice in energy efficient design, the selection and sizing of energy-efficient plant and equipment, systems and other energy infrastructure

- maintain all plant and equipment, and control and manage systems and energy infrastructure in such a way as to minimise energy wastage

- monitor and report on the Company's energy consumption and identify and implement opportunities for improved energy efficiency

- pursue the use of renewable and alternative energy sources to supplement conventional energy sources

- address our obligations as a member of the global community including legislative requirements and minimising our impact on the environment

- strive to procure, distribute and maintain energy resources at the lowest cost whilst addressing the items above.

Our corporate objective is therefore to manage our energy usage and resources as efficiently as possible so as to minimise waste.

To help ensure we give proper consideration to our energy management and environmental responsibilities, this Policy will be implemented, monitored and enforced throughout the workplace. All staff are expected to work towards the aims of this Policy and co-operate with management in its execution.

2. Implementation

In order to achieve our desired aims, the Policy will be implemented and achieved by:

- purchasing fuel, energy supplies and other utilities at the most economic cost

- reducing the amount of pollution, particularly CO_2 emissions, caused by inefficient energy consumption

- undertaking regular energy audits - these are best carried out by professional consultants, though some electricity companies provide them free of charge. Simple audits can be carried out in-house by measuring compliance with energy saving options or by using systems such as http://www.green-office.org.uk/audit.php

- investing in a continuous programme of energy-saving measures to reduce energy consumption

- safeguarding the achieved reductions by continually monitoring Performance Indicators

- raising the awareness of employees on energy conservation matters with the co-operation of all stakeholders

- determining areas which would benefit from sub-metering and ensuring such meters are installed

- undertaking benchmarking to ensure worst performers can be targeted and year-on-year usages can be assessed

- having energy consumption data available for all buildings - this can be collected by monitoring energy usage within each building by monitoring and recording the units of electricity and gas used

- reviewing routine maintenance, including major replacements against an energy efficiency checklist to ensure that opportunities to switch fuels, install controls or improve thermal standards etc. are taken

- benchmarking all new construction against the BREEAM standards - see http://www. breeam.org for more information

- ensuring equipment purchasing policies consider energy consumption for the purchase of all items of equipment and be fully compliant with current best practice

- considering new technologies such as renewable energy, high efficiency motors etc. where appropriate.

The Carbon Trust provides free surveys to organisations with energy bills greater than £50,000 per year. Smaller companies (energy bills under £50,000 per year) can also benefit from advice over the phone by calling the Carbon Trust Helpline on 0800 085 2005. Visit the following site for more information:

http://www.thecarbontrust.co.uk/energy/assessyourorganisation/energy_survey.htm

Guidance note - energy efficiency

Do you know how efficient your machinery is, or what temperature your heating thermostat is set at? Checking and changing settings may help you make significant financial savings and minimise your environmental impact.

IMPROVE YOUR EFFICIENCY

In addition to the development and implementation of a corporate Energy Management Policy, you need to consider what practical steps you can take to reduce and control the level of energy usage. We have, therefore, included a **Guidance Note - Energy Efficiency** with a wide range of tips and suggestions that can be implemented to help you conserve and reduce your consumption. This guidance also includes links to websites that we feel may help you.

GUIDANCE NOTE -
ENERGY EFFICIENCY

It is easy to save electricity and therefore money! The simplest ways can be by simply turning off the lights, computers, televisions and other electrical equipment when not in use. Leaving a television or DVD player on stand-by still uses a considerable amount of electricity.

Top tips for saving energy

There are many ways to save energy and to be more efficient in your use of electricity. The following energy saving tips can help to reduce fuel bills at little or no cost.

Curtains

- at night, close curtains to stop heat being lost through windows. Take care not to drape curtains over radiators as this will funnel heat straight out of the windows.

Heating

- turning down the central heating thermostat by 1°C can cut as much as 10% off your annual heating bills. Considerable savings can also be made on the running costs by heating your property for an hour less each day.

Water

- remember not to set the thermostat too high on your water heater; 60°C/140°F is usually sufficient for most purposes

- have a shower instead of a bath if you have one and you'll save time, money and water

- always put the plug in your basin or sink - leaving hot water taps running is both wasteful and expensive. If you have a dripping tap ensure it is repaired quickly. In just one day, enough hot water to fill a bath can be lost down the drain.

Lights

- always turn off lights when you leave a room for long periods

- use low energy light bulbs wherever you can as they use less than a quarter of the electricity used by ordinary light bulbs and can last up to 15 times longer.

Television and hi-fi equipment

- switch off your TV, DVD player and hi-fi equipment. Leaving such equipment on standby can use between 10 and 60% of the electricity that would be used if the device were left on.

Fridges and freezers

- defrost fridges and freezers regularly to help keep them running efficiently

- don't put hot or warm food straight into the fridge - let it cool down first, otherwise the fridge needs to work harder to compensate for the increased temperature within it

- where possible, position your fridge or freezer away from cookers or heaters

- don't keep opening the fridge door. Each time you do this the fridge loses some energy.

Washing machines

- where possible wait until you have a full load before using your washing machine, alternatively, use the half-load or economy setting

- modern washing detergents and machines work just as well at lower temperatures, so think twice before selecting a boil wash.

Hot water cylinder jacket

- putting a lagging jacket around your hot water tank and insulating hot water pipes can pay for itself in a few months and go on saving you money for years to come.

Loft insulation

- if you are prepared to invest more in making your property energy efficient, loft insulation can help you reduce your fuel bills significantly. Up to 25% of heat loss occurs through roof spaces which are not insulated. Insulation can therefore pay for itself through lower energy bills, making sound economic sense. A minimum thickness of 250mm glass fibre or mineral wool is recommended. In some cases grants may also be available from your local authority.

Cavity wall insulation

- insulation can be put into cavity walls which can save up to 35% of heat loss.

Guidance note - alternative energy

Over the last few years a number of alternative sources of energy have come onto the market. In our guidance document we've outlined how these technologies work, and how you could use them within your business.

ALTERNATIVE ENERGY

In our **Guidance Note - Alternative Energy** we have looked at a number of alternative forms of energy that are available for the generation of electricity. These have many environmental benefits and the potential to cut costs compared to your traditional energy bills.

Note. Before taking the plunge into these technologies, it's well worthwhile doing your homework first. Many people have purchased these products only to find out later that they aren't as good as they'd hoped.

Example. Although wind turbines are a relatively cheap option, they need a constant strong wind to generate any power. So if your building is in the middle of a built-up area, the chances of your turbine getting the wind it needs is limited.

GUIDANCE NOTE -
ALTERNATIVE ENERGY

Forecasts and geological surveys suggest that there may only be enough oil for another 30 years usage, natural gas for 50 years, and coal for 200 years.

Whilst there is no immediate shortage, it is inevitable that prices will rise and availability will become more and more of an issue. Organisations therefore need to give careful consideration to their use of energy, ensuring that they do not needlessly waste it.

However, in addition to the traditional fossil fuels, other forms of electricity are now becoming available. These are called renewable energy sources because they are generated by sources of energy that will never run out. Some of the renewable energy sources are outlined below:

Solar power

The energy from the sun can be used to heat water in solar panels and to generate electricity. To produce electricity you need photovoltaic (PV) solar panels, which are a much more expensive option than for solar water heating.

Solar heating panels are designed to absorb the sun's heat. They contain water which, once hot, travels through a coil within the hot water cylinder. This transfers the heat to the water within the cylinder and is known as an "indirect" system. In "direct" systems, water from the panels goes straight into the cylinder - these are not suitable for areas with very hard water.

Photovoltaic cells use a completely different technology to generate electricity.

Solar power, like many other renewable energy sources, doesn't produce carbon dioxide or harm the environment. The ideal location for solar panels is a south-facing roof clear of obstructions and shadows. Due to the nature of the British climate, solar power should not be relied upon as the sole source of heating or electricity, but as a secondary or supplementary source.

The Low Carbon Buildings programme has been established specifically to provide grants for microgeneration technologies for householders, community organisations, schools, the public sector and businesses. Microgeneration is the stand-alone generation of low carbon heat and/or electricity which, for example, could be through solar power, micro wind turbines and other forms of alternative energy. The following website provides further details on the Low Carbon Buildings programme:

http://www.est.org.uk/housingbuildings/funding/lowcarbonbuildings/

Wind power

Wind turbines can be used to harness the power of the wind to generate electricity. Wind power is one of the most popular forms of renewable energy and wind farms have appeared in many parts of the UK. One of the newer developments in wind power is that of the micro wind turbine which can be used by individual homeowners and businesses to generate their own electricity. As with solar power, grants are available in some areas for the installation of micro wind turbines.

Hydro-electricity

This means using moving water to turn turbines and make electricity. It is more common in countries with a lot of rivers and mountains such as Norway and Scotland. Hydro-electric schemes generally involve massive construction projects that are implemented over a long period of time. A major hydro-electric scheme can take between ten and 20 years from conception to completion.

Wave power

Wave power can be generated by placing turbines into the sea that use either the up and down motion of the sea, or the tidal motion to generate electricity. It has been estimated that in the UK alone the recoverable wave energy resources exceed the total UK electricity demand. This makes wave power an attractive option for the future.

Waste power

Energy from waste facilities can be used to generate both electricity and heat/hot water by burning waste and rubbish from industrial, agricultural and domestic sources. This has the added benefit that the waste doesn't get disposed of in landfill. The only problem is getting enough waste to keep the incinerators working.

Green electricity supply

The UK has the largest potential for renewable energy within Europe. By choosing to purchase green energy, businesses can also reduce the environmental impact of traditional energy generation and support the renewable power industry at the same time. Following the deregulation of electricity supply it became possible to receive electricity from suppliers that generate or trade green energy.

Many electricity suppliers now offer a green tariff which guarantees that the electricity you purchase comes from renewable sources as opposed to traditional fossil fuels. This is generally in response to the government's target of producing 10% of the UK's electricity from renewable sources by 2010. To encourage the take up of green electricity the government taxes businesses under the Climate Change Levy for any gas and electricity they use. However you are exempt from this tax if you can show, with Levy Exemption Certificates, that the electricity purchased came from renewable sources.

Signing up to a green tariff does not guarantee you get direct green electricity down the wire into your office, but that somewhere within the grid the demand for electricity is being matched by an equivalent supply of green electricity.

There are two main types of green electricity tariff:

- **Energy tariffs.** These suppliers promise to buy renewable energy to match the equivalent of your electricity demand. They may also sell green energy to other suppliers.

- **Fund tariffs.** These suppliers put money aside to fund projects to increase awareness of environmental or energy issues. Contributions are deducted from your bill either at a fixed rate or in the form of a premium.

- **Combination.** You can also buy a combination of the two. These are the most common tariffs and are generally considered to be better because not only is the demand for green energy being matched, but contributions to a fund are made as well. This has the added benefit of encouraging electricity generators to produce more green electricity.

  For more information on which green electric tariffs are available in your area, have a look at the following website, or contact your current supplier:

  http://www.greenelectricity.org

Office - energy saving checklist

As the costs of energy continue to rise it's important for businesses to reduce consumption by as much as possible. Our checklist provides some suggestions on how to achieve this in an office environment.

USING OUR CHECKLIST

Our checklist asks you to take stock of current energy usage and to address the resulting issues, with the aim of making savings. You should record your results from the questions asked and then use these to develop an action plan. At the end of each section we have provided you with additional guidance to help you do this.

THREE ENERGY-SAVING AREAS

The document is divided into three sections. The first deals with heating and asks questions that relate to controlling room temperatures so that heating systems are being used in the most economical manner. The second section deals with office lighting and how it is controlled. Guidance is given on types of lamp that use less electricity plus advice on methods of lighting control. The final part of our checklist asks questions about office equipment, and here we suggest ways that you can reduce energy consumption with computers, printers, copiers etc.

OFFICE - ENERGY SAVING CHECKLIST

Use the checklist to establish where you are at present and then formulate action plans to make savings. The questionnaire is divided into three separate parts: Heating, Lighting and Office equipment, and you need to consider all three in order to make savings.

Heating

Item	Result
What is the present office temperature?	
Do staff complain about the temperature - too hot, too cold?	
Have heaters/boilers been serviced in the last twelve months?	
Are portable heaters used to supplement the existing heating system?	
Are heaters and air conditioning units operating in the same area?	
Do all areas need to be heated fully, e.g. storerooms, toilets, etc?	
Are there room thermostats that work, and are they set to the correct temperature?	
Are all timers on heating systems working and set to the correct times?	
Are there any obstructions in front of radiators or heaters?	
How are extractor fans controlled?	
Are windows and doors open when heating or air conditioning is on?	
Is there any cold coming in from draughty windows and doors?	
How hot is the hot water?	

If rooms are too hot or heated unnecessarily this is easy to deal with by altering timers and/or thermostats. Improving insulation and draught control can also significantly reduce energy consumption. Poorly maintained boilers can add 30% to heating costs.

Portable heaters are expensive so only use if essential and only for short periods (use a timer switch).

Many people complain of being too hot at work, so make sure that thermostats are set at 19–20°c, and install thermostatic radiator valves where possible. Turn the heating down or off rather than opening windows. Timers need to be set so heating is only on when needed, i.e. when the building is occupied. Note. Some degree of frost protection will be required during winter months so ensure that a frost thermostat is fitted to heating systems.

Lighting

Item	Result
Are lights switched off when rooms are unoccupied?	
Are large diameter fluorescent tube lights still used?	
Are lamps, fittings, windows and roof lights kept clean?	
Are light bulbs long life, or are traditional tungsten light bulbs still used?	
Are light switches easy to find and labelled with reminders to switch off etc?	
Are external lights controlled by a timer or photoelectric cell?	

Energy-efficient lighting can save your business hundreds of pounds a year. Old large diameter (38mm) fluorescent tubes use 10% more energy than slimline tubes (26mm diameter), and new high frequency fluorescent lighting extends lamp life and can reduce consumption by up to a quarter. Dirt reduces lighting levels by a surprising amount. Standard filament bulbs are very expensive to run and actually produce more heat than light. Compact fluorescent bulbs have a longer life and use up to 75% less energy. Local task lighting is more pleasant to work with as it reduces glare and electricity bills at the same time. Keeping windows clean allows more natural light and can reduce the need for artificial lighting. Encourage staff to turn off lights in unoccupied rooms.

Office equipment

Item	Result
Do computers have built-in energy-saving features, and if so are they activated?	
Are computers left on overnight?	
Are monitors switched off when not in use?	
Are photocopiers and other equipment energy efficient?	
Are photocopiers located near air conditioned areas or air conditioning units?	
Are printers and photocopiers left on overnight/at weekends?	
Are vending machines/water coolers etc. left on permanently?	
Can you see any other obvious wastes of energy?	

Survey your existing office equipment based on the questions above and plan to make changes where necessary. And don't forget to educate your staff on energy reduction techniques such as turning off equipment rather than letting it remain on stand-by.

Register of environmental legislation - energy

This part of our Register of Environmental Legislation covers the energy legislation most likely to affect you if you're based in England.

WHEN AND HOW TO USE THE DOCUMENT

Each register includes four columns: the legislation title; a summary of the law; the regulator's name and details of how you're affected. The first three columns are pre-filled with relevant information. All you need to do is fill in the last one with an explanation of how the legislation impacts your business. We've even provided some examples to get you started. Completing the register will provide a way to self-check compliance, and it's also a document which you can show to inspectors, auditors and clients to demonstrate that you're following good practice.

WHAT'S COVERED?

Our energy legislation register covers a wide spectrum, including climate change and carbon taxes, energy requirements for buildings and product design.

REGISTER OF ENVIRONMENTAL LEGISLATION - ENERGY

Introduction

The Environmental Management Standard ISO 14001 recommends that each organisation "establishes and maintains a procedure to identify and have access to legal and other requirements to which the organisation subscribes, that are applicable to the environmental aspects of its activities, products or services."

It is the purpose of this register of environmental legislation to demonstrate compliance with this standard.

Energy

(**Note.** *This table lists the most commonly applicable legislation relating to energy use in small and medium sized businesses (SMEs). Delete and amend as required and complete the "Aspects of activities affected" column as appropriate to your business. It should be noted that the Energy Acts 2008 and 2010, Planning Act 2008 and Climate Change Act 2008, are not included due to the limited direct impact on SMEs.*)

Legislation	Summary	Regulator	Aspects of activities affected (Describe how and why the legislation affects you. Refer to associated internal documents)
Climate Change Levy	Introduces a tax on energy supplied to industry, commerce, agriculture, the public sector and other services. The levy is charged on the industrial and commercial supply of taxable commodities for lighting, heating and power including gas, petroleum, electricity and coal. The levy does not apply to taxable commodities used by domestic consumers, or by charities for non-business use. Businesses who make or intend to make taxable supplies, must register with HM Revenue & Customs for the Climate Change Levy.	HM Revenue & Customs	*e.g. As we are coal merchant supplying business premises we have registered and the copy of our registration is held by ......(insert name).*
Carbon Reduction Commitment Order 2010	Requires businesses with half-hourly metering (HMM) of their electrical consumption to register with the Environment Agency and if their consumption exceeds certain amounts, to report their energy consumption to the Environment Agency (EA). The biggest users must buy "carbon credits".	EA	*e.g. We have a half-hourly meter and our aggregated HHM electrical consumption exceeds 3,000MWH but is below 6,000MWH. Therefore, we have registered with the EA and annually report our HHM energy consumption.*

Legislation	Summary	Regulator	Aspects of activities affected (Describe how and why the legislation affects you. Refer to associated internal documents)
Buildings Regulations 2000 Part L	Introduces requirements for energy efficiency of buildings and for builders to calculate and display energy ratings on new or altered buildings. From October 2010, any new building constructed must produce 25% less carbon emissions compared with the previous standard.	Local authorities	*e.g. We are not a builder and are therefore not directly affected by the legislation. However, we have noted the building energy rating information and implemented plans to improve the efficiency of our building.*
Energy Performance of Buildings (Certificates and Inspections) (England and Wales) Regulations 2007, as amended	Requires building owners to make an energy performance certificate available for buyers or tenants and to inspect air conditioning systems regularly. Also requires public buildings to have a display energy certificate on show within the building.	Local authorities	
Requirements associated with planning permissions	Under the Planning and Energy Act 2008, local planning authorities can set requirements for energy use and energy efficiency.	Local authorities	
Town and Country Planning Act 1990 and associated legislation	Planning permission required for certain alterations to buildings. Required when introducing certain improvements for environmental reasons, e.g. solar panels, wind turbines etc.	Local authorities	

Legislation	Summary	Regulator	Aspects of activities affected (Describe how and why the legislation affects you. Refer to associated internal documents)
The Ecodesign for Energy-Using Products Regulations 2007, as amended	Implement requirements of Directive 2005/32/EC of the European Parliament and of the Council establishing a framework for the setting of eco-design requirements for energy-using product. Products listed in Schedule 1 of the Regulations must meet the standards set out.	National Measurement Office	e.g. Our business does not design, make or import products listed in these regulations. However, we take into account energy efficiency and other eco-design issues within our purchasing process.
Energy Information Regulations - various regulations affecting domestic appliances, e.g. fridges, freezers, lamps, washing machines, tumble dryers, dishwashers etc.	Requires suppliers of household appliances affected to provide energy consumption information on their products, and dealers to display this information to potential buyers.	Local authorities	e.g. We do not have duties under these regulations. However, we take into account energy efficiency and other eco-design issues within our purchasing process.
EU Regulation on a Revised Community Eco-Label Award Scheme 1980/2000	Sets out a scheme to award an "eco-label" to manufacturers who want to inform consumers about what they are doing to reduce the environmental impact of their products.	Trading Standards	

Legislation	Summary	Regulator	Aspects of activities affected (Describe how and why the legislation affects you. Refer to associated internal documents)
EU Regulation on ecodesign requirements for non-directional household lamps 244/2009	Lists requirements for marketing fluorescent lamps, high intensity discharge lamps, ballasts and luminaires. Also includes benchmarks for office lighting and public street lighting products.	Trading Standards	
EU Regulation on Eco-design requirements for lamps 347/2010	Establishes eco-design requirements for marketing non-directional household lamps including those marketed for non-household use.	Trading Standards	
EU Regulation 1222/2009 on the labelling of tyres with respect to fuel efficiency and other essential parameters	Requires tyre suppliers to ensure that the tyres they deliver to distributors and end users are labelled with their fuel efficiency and noise levels from November 1 2012.	Trading Standards	

Chapter 9

Environmental
impact assessments

Guidance note - environmental impact/risk assessments

An environmental impact assessment is a way of considering the potential environmental effects of a proposed activity or development. It's a very complicated process and is one that's usually completed by an environmental consultant or specialist.

ENVIRONMENTAL IMPACT ASSESSMENTS

Environmental impact assessments (EIA) help to inform the appropriate authorities and those responsible for the proposal the impact an activity is likely to have on the environment. An EIA is required under UK legislation for all major developments with the potential to cause large-scale environmental disruption or which may have a significant impact on the environment. To help you identify what needs to be assessed we've produced a **Guidance Note - Environmental Impact/Risk Assessments**, which identifies the key stages in the process, including recognition of potential hazards, possible consequences and the significance of a risk.

GUIDANCE NOTE -
ENVIRONMENTAL IMPACT/RISK ASSESSMENTS

A key element of the **Environmental Protection Act 1990** is to identify the impacts our business operations have on our surrounding environment. These impacts should be assessed prior to the commencement of any operations which may have an adverse effect on the environment. These assessments will be monitored and reviewed on an annual basis and amended where appropriate to cater for the requirements of specific projects.

All senior managers should consider the impact their operations have on the environment and raise a formal environmental risk assessment.

Sub-contractors and other staff should be made aware of any assessments that have been undertaken to address the activities they are carrying out. Any actions that are required to keep these assessments valid and relevant must then be followed.

The basic stages to be adopted when carrying out an environmental risk assessment are as follows:

Stage 1: Hazard identification

Guidance defines a *hazard* as a "property or situation that in particular circumstances could lead to harm". This may be determined by properties or circumstances and could include, for example, the release of chlorofluorocarbons (CFCs); a tidal surge along a stretch of the coast; a dry summer leading to low river flows; or the planting of a genetically modified crop. Where risk assessments are to be applied, the hazards may be as broad as the adverse impact of road transport on the environment, or the adverse impact of induced climate change from the contribution of fossil fuel-derived carbon dioxide emissions.

The identification of relevant hazards will therefore have an important bearing on the overall assessment and the credibility of the final assessment.

One common pitfall in establishing the hazards is to overlook secondary hazards that may arise. For example, during a river flood, sediments may be deposited within the working area. If these sediments were to be contaminated, they might pose an additional hazard.

Stage 2: Identification of consequences

The potential consequences that may arise from any given hazard are inherent in that hazard. Although the full range of potential consequences must be considered at this stage, no account is taken of likely exposure and therefore likely consequences. For example, while the potential consequences of a discharge of toxic metals to a watercourse may be self-evident, a flood may have additional, non-obvious consequences such as pollution arising from an over-stretched sewerage system, or loss of habitats due to river scouring.

These examples help to highlight why it is necessary to take a broad look at the potential environmental damage that may occur, if only to be clear why some potential consequences are rejected for further assessment.

Stage 3: Estimation of the severity of consequences

The consequences of a particular hazard may be actual or potential harm to human health, property or the natural environment. The severity of such consequences can be determined in different ways depending on whether they are being considered as part of a risk screening process, or as part of a more detailed quantification of risk. At all stages of risk assessment several key features need to be considered, as described below.

Spatial scale of the consequences

The geographical scale of harm resulting from an environmental impact will often extend considerably beyond the boundaries of the source of the hazard. Failure to consider this at an early stage may result in the scope of the risk assessment being too limited. For example, a major accident in a chemical plant is likely to have significant effects on the environment well beyond the perimeter of the site.

Temporal scale of the consequences

The duration of the harm that results may be so prolonged that the damage can be assumed to be permanent and the environment beyond recovery. For example, the release of a genetically modified crop could result in extensive cross-breeding with adjacent indigenous flora, any harmful environmental impacts could extend far into the future.

Time to onset of the consequences

A further factor to consider is how quickly harmful effects might be seen. Standard economic techniques tend to discount impacts that will happen in the future but sustainable development emphasises the need to protect the interests of future generations. Risk assessment and management must therefore pay as much attention to long-term problems as to the more immediate risks. For example, the spillage of a solvent on porous ground may not result in an impact on the underlying aquifer for decades. However, once realised, the duration of the harm is likely to be of the order of decades and will compromise the value of that aquifer as a source of water for future generations.

Stage 4: Estimation of the probability of the consequences

The above stages have assumed that realisation of the hazard will lead to environmental harm. However, the probability or likelihood of the consequences occurring must also be taken into account.

This has three components:

- the probability of the hazard occurring

- the probability of the receptors being exposed to the hazard

- the probability of harm resulting from exposure to the hazard.

Stage 5: Evaluating the significance of a risk

Having determined the likelihood and severity of the consequences that may arise as a result of the hazard, it is important to place them in some sort of context. It is at this point that some value judgements are made, either through reference to some pre-existing measure, such as an environmental quality or flood defence standard, or by reference to social, ethical, or political standards.

Options appraisal

Having estimated the magnitude and the significance of the risks posed by the hazard(s), the options for risk management are identified and evaluated. It is important to carry out this procedure as a distinct preliminary step because ill-considered risk management strategies may otherwise result in wasted effort and expenditure on the part of the decision-maker. The options commonly available are:

- exploring the acceptability, or otherwise, of the risk - this can include rejecting unacceptable risks altogether or accepting the risk being imposed

- reducing the hazard through new technology, procedures or investment or

- mitigating the effects, through improved environmental management techniques.

The decision on precisely which option or combination of options to choose will involve a balance of risk reduction, costs, benefits and social considerations.

Guidance note - identifying
contaminated land

Wouldn't it be good if contaminated land had a big sign on it to identify what the contamination is and what needs to be done to remove it? However, this is never the case, often detailed sampling and testing is required.

IDENTIFYING CONTAMINATED LAND

One of the most common hazards found in an environmental impact assessment is contaminated land. This is a particularly technical subject and one which will usually require the services of a consultant. But to help you understand the basic principles we've produced a **Guidance Note - Identifying Contaminated Land** that describes the legislative framework which sets out what's needed to treat it and what a consultant is likely to do to identify the full extent of the contamination.

GUIDANCE NOTE -
IDENTIFYING CONTAMINATED LAND

Contaminated land is land that has been contaminated by substances in quantities sufficient to cause harm or damage to humans, animals or the environment.

Any land that contains substances at above their "natural" concentration levels can be defined as "contaminated". However, this definition would include most land within any urban areas, as well as large proportions of farmland. Contamination caused by previous industrial uses and the disposal of waste can also occur. Therefore, in order to give a sense of proportion, the assessment of contaminated land is balanced against its potential to cause harm in terms of risks to human health/environmental receptors and/or pollution of controlled waters.

The **Environment Act 1995** provides the current statutory framework for dealing with contaminated land. The regime is based on the identification and remediation of contaminated land and gives a statutory definition based on the risks of significant harm to specified receptors or pollution of controlled waters. The precise definition in the Act is *"any land which appears to the local authority in whose area it is situated to be in such a condition, by reason of substances in, on or under the land, that (a) significant harm is being caused or there is a significant possibility of such harm being caused, or (b) pollution of controlled waters is being, or is likely to be, caused"*.

At significant levels, contaminants can not only affect our health, but also cause damage to buildings by attacking concrete foundations. In addition to physical risks, the matter of blight can't be ignored. Pollution is an emotive issue, and the talk of contamination can destroy property values, even when the actual presence of it is slight.

Site investigations and soil surveys should always be carried out by environmental experts/geotechnical engineers. The investigation should establish what contaminants are present, their concentration levels and whether they are inert or mobile. With mobile contaminants, some will have definite paths, such as radon gas or methane, which as a vapour will be heading to the surface. Other substances, such as leachates, can migrate through the ground causing pollution of the groundwater. The investigation should also consider these issues.

Site investigations and soil surveys

The purpose of the site investigation should be to first identify the potential for contamination and then identify possible areas that may require remedial works in order to make a site "suitable for use". Site investigations are generally carried out in three stages, depending on the complexity and scope of any contamination. The adoption of a staged approach enables resources to be more accurately targeted where it is likely that contamination exists.

Definition of "suitable for use"

The "suitable for use" principle means that remediation (clean-up) measures are required where there are unacceptable risks to human health or the environment (including flora and fauna) arising from the actual or proposed use of the site. Therefore a site-specific assessment of the risks presented by a site must be undertaken in order to determine the extent of any required remedial works.

Site investigations

Stage 1 - desktop/scoping study

The desktop/scoping study involves the collection of historic information about the site and its past uses. This model considers all potential contaminant/pollution sources, pathways and receptors. The report should document the site history and identify all potential sources of contamination back to when it was a green field site. Where necessary, baseline studies should be carried out and samples extracted and tested to establish what contaminants are present. The conclusions of the report should contain the results of all studies and tests and make recommendations for any additional studies/testing required during Stage 2.

Suggested contents for desktop/scoping study reports

- purpose and aims of study
- site location and layout plans appropriately scaled and annotated
- appraisal of site history
- appraisal of site walkover survey
- assessment of environmental setting, to include:
  - geology, hydrogeology, hydrology
  - information on coal workings (if appropriate)
  - information from Environment Agency on abstractions, pollution incidents, water quality classification, landfill sites within 250m, etc.
  - assessment of current/proposed site use and surrounding land uses
  - review of any previous site contamination studies (desk-based or intrusive) or remediation works.

Preliminary (qualitative) assessment of risks, to include:

- appraisal of potential contaminant sources, pathways, and receptors (pollutant linkages).

Recommendations for intrusive contamination investigation (if necessary) to include identification of target areas for more detailed investigation.

Stage 2 - detailed investigation

Following the scoping study, the "Detailed Investigation" stage will involve more intrusive investigations, comprehensive soil testing and the preparation of quantitative risk assessments based on the findings of the tests and surveys. The Stage 2 study should also include recommendations for appropriate remediation options, where applicable.

Suggested contents for detailed investigation reports

- review of any previous site investigation contamination studies (desk-based or intrusive) or remediation works
- site investigation methodology, to include:
  - plan showing exploration locations, on site structures, above/below ground storage tanks, etc. and to be appropriately scaled and annotated
  - justification of exploration locations
  - sampling and analytical strategies
  - borehole/trial pit logs.
- results and findings of investigation, to include:
  - ground conditions (soil and groundwater regimes, including made ground)
  - discussion of soil/groundwater/surface water contamination (visual, olfactory, analytical).
- conceptual site model
- risk assessment - Based on contaminant source - pathway - receptor model (to assess the consequences and likelihood of occurrence). Details of the site specific risk assessment model selected and the justification in its selection and use should be stated
- recommendations for remediation should include all relevant information which should follow the "suitable for use" approach - based both on the current use and circumstances of the land and its proposed new use
- recommendations for further investigation if necessary.

Stage 3 - remediation strategy/validation report

There are typically two distinct stages involved in the remediation of land, the first being the preparation and submission of a "Remediation Statement" to the local authority for their approval. This must be submitted and approved before the commencement of any site works and the document should detail the objectives, methodology and procedures of the proposed remediation works. The second stage follows the completion of the works where a "Validation Report" must be prepared demonstrating that the works have been carried out satisfactorily and remediation targets have been achieved.

Suggested contents for remediation statements

- objectives of the remediation works
- details of the remedial works to be carried out, to include:
  - description of ground conditions (soil and groundwater)
  - type, form and scale of contamination to be remediated
  - remediation methodology
  - site plans/drawings
  - phasing of works and approximate timescales
  - consents and licences, e.g. discharge consents, waste management licence, asbestos waste material removal licence, etc.
  - site management measures to protect neighbours
- details of how the works will be validated to ensure the remediation objectives have been met, to include:
  - sampling strategy
  - use of on-site observations, visual/olfactory evidence
  - chemical analysis
  - proposed clean-up standards (i.e. contaminant concentration).

Suggested contents for validation reports

As for remediation statements, plus:

- details of who carried out the work
- details and justification of any changes from original remediation statement
- substantiating data - should include where appropriate:
  - laboratory and in-situ test results
  - monitoring for groundwater and gases
  - summary data plots and tables relating to clean-up criteria
  - plans showing treatment areas and details of any differences from the original remediation statement
  - waste management documentation
- confirmation that remediation objectives have been met.

For more detailed information on the management of contaminated land, the Environment Agency has produced a publication entitled: "Model Procedures for the Management of Contaminated Land", this can be freely downloaded from the following web page:

http://publications.environment-agency.gov.uk/pdf/SCHO0804BIBR-e-e.pdf

Guidance note - contaminated land

and tax relief

To help organisations meet the clean-up costs associated with the development of brown field sites, the government has introduced a system of tax relief which enables companies to offset the remediation costs against their tax liabilities.

TAX RELIEF SCHEME

To help you make the most of the contaminated land tax relief scheme, we've produced a **Guidance Note - Contaminated Land and Tax Relief**. It details the qualifying factors that make land eligible under the scheme and when you're entitled to claim tax relief.

Further, detailed information on this is available from the HMRC website: http://www.hmrc.gov.uk/manuals/cirdmanual/CIRD60080.htm

GUIDANCE NOTE -
CONTAMINATED LAND AND TAX RELIEF

Businesses can claim tax relief of up to 150% of the qualifying clean-up costs for any remediation work undertaken to clean up contaminated land.

Land qualifies if all of the following are true:

- the land is in the UK and was acquired by the company to carry out its trade or property letting business

- the land was contaminated at the time it was acquired

- the contamination was not caused by the actions or inactions of the company or a person with a relevant connection to the company.

Land includes any buildings or other premises on it.

Land is contaminated if there is a substance in, on or under it that has the potential to do harm to humans, ecosystems or water sources. A substance means a chemical element or one of its compounds, whether solid, liquid or gas.

The relief is only available to businesses subject to Corporation Tax, not to individuals or partnerships. Businesses responsible for polluting the land or adding to existing contamination are not eligible for the relief.

The money spent on remediation works, i.e. cleaning up land, qualifies if:

- it is spent on land which is contaminated

- it is spent on qualifying land remediation

- it is spent on paying employees or sub-contractors, or on buying materials

- it would not have been spent if the land wasn't contaminated

- the cost was not met directly or indirectly by anyone else.

Further details can be obtained from the following website:

http://www.hmrc.gov.uk/manuals/cirdmanual/CIRD60000.htm

Guidance note - contaminated land
remediation techniques

If you have, or are intending to purchase, land that you know to be contaminated, then you'll need to remediate the land. This can be achieved in a number of ways - all of which are detailed in our guidance document.

PRINCIPAL TECHNIQUES OF LAND REMEDIATION

Contaminated land remediation can be extremely complicated and should only be carried out by specialist contractors. But to help you to gain a better understanding of the principal techniques available, we've produced a **Guidance Note - Contaminated Land Remediation Techniques**. This outlines the main commercial techniques adopted in the UK for the remediation of contaminated land. This information is especially useful when making initial enquiries about specialist contractors and consultants.

GUIDANCE NOTE -
CONTAMINATED LAND REMEDIATION TECHNIQUES

The treatment of contaminated land is a highly specialised process that should only be carried out by contractors with the appropriate experience, knowledge and resources. Many land remediation projects will also require a licence to be issued by the Environment Agency.

Whereas historically the only effective option was for contaminated land to be excavated, removed from site and then refilled with fresh uncontaminated topsoil, or a similar hard surface where applicable, there is today a wide range of more cost-effective and innovative solutions. Also where contaminated land is to be removed and transported off site, then the **Hazardous Waste Regulations** would apply.

Flushing away contaminants with water or other chemicals can also be performed in some cases, while vacuum suction treatment can be used to remove petrol and other volatile pollutants, if, for example, work is to be carried out on a former fuel storage site.

Bio-remediation

Bio-remediation is the treatment of contaminated material involving the natural degradation of contaminants by bacteria. This process is particularly suitable for hydrocarbon contaminants such as petrol and diesel range organics and other carcinogenic hydrocarbons such as benzene. The rate of decomposition can be greatly increased by the addition of nutrients and by controlling moisture, temperature, oxygen and pH levels. Metals like lead and iron cannot be treated with these methods.

Containment

If the contamination cannot be taken out of the soil economically, an impervious liner or capping material can often be used to seal and contain it within the ground. This, however, is not suitable where pollution of the groundwater, or migration of gases could occur, or where a risk of the material being disturbed in the future exists. Comprehensive and accurate records of the location of all contaminated material must be maintained and the facility for the ongoing monitoring of the contamination may be required.

Soil washing

Soil washing can be very effective on a wide range of contaminants in granular or coarse grained material if works on the principle that contamination forms a surface coating on the soil particles.

Soils of different particle sizes are separated before treatment using a variety of processes such as high pressure washing, attrition scrubbing and centrifuges. Granular material, once treated, can then be processed and re-used on site. One of the major benefits of this technique is that only a relatively small amount of finer silty materials which contain a high level of contamination, needs to be removed and disposed of, off site.

Soil washing is particularly effective in reducing the amount of material disposed of at landfill sites, reducing the cost of both disposal and any imported backfill material that is required.

Soil stabilisation

Soil stabilisation and modification is a well practised technique that involves the addition of lime and/or cement to the soil. Lime modifies the structure of the soil and the moisture content of cohesive soils is reduced, leading to considerable improvement in bearing capacity. This technique is a relatively low-cost and an effective alternative to the importing of aggregates for both temporary and permanent works.

With contaminated soils, the cement mixed with the soil solidifies around the soil particles when it reacts with water forming a physical bond that contains the contaminants. The solidification process also lowers the permeability of treated material, inhibiting the movement of water thus preventing leaching.

These are the most common forms of land remediation, though many other specialised techniques are also available. A specialist contractor/consultant should be consulted for advice on any land remediation works.

Guidance note - contaminated land
emergency control procedure

If you identify, or even suspect, that land may be contaminated, both you and your staff need to know what actions to take. The best way of achieving this is to have a formal policy in place.

EMERGENCY CONTROL PROCEDURES

Where contaminated land is known to exist, the risks and hazards can vary significantly, ranging from life threatening to humans or flora/fauna, to having a negligible impact on the natural environment. It's therefore important to establish exactly what risks are presented by the contamination. Strict procedures and controls must be adopted when working in the vicinity of contaminated land; to assist you use our **Guidance Note - Contaminated Land Emergency Control Procedure**.

GUIDANCE NOTE -
CONTAMINATED LAND EMERGENCY CONTROL PROCEDURE

1. All operations involving contaminated land must be clearly identified and project specific risk assessments and method statements must be prepared.

2. If contaminated materials are stored on site, the method of containment must prevent any escape of dust, leachate or other substances.

3. Disposal of contaminated materials off site must be to licensed sites and in accordance with the duty of care.

4. When dealing with known contaminated land, and run-off is becoming a problem, control procedures for the prevention of water pollution, such as the use of absorbent spill kits, bunds and drain covers must be implemented.

5. When dealing with known contaminated land and dust generation is becoming a problem, control procedures for the prevention of air pollution, such as the use of dampening techniques, must be implemented.

6. In addition, all operatives in the area must be issued with dust masks to prevent ingestion of the contaminated materials.

7. If it is suspected that contaminated/polluted land has been discovered, stop work immediately, seal off the area, and report the discovery to the Site Manager. The following may give an indication that contamination has been found:

   - discoloured or oily soil (chemical or oil residues)

   - the soil has a fibrous texture (asbestos)

   - presence of foreign objects (chemical/oil containers)

   - evidence of underground structures and storage tanks

   - existence of waste pits

   - old drain runs and contamination within building and tanks.

8. Suspected contaminated materials must be tested at an approved laboratory to ascertain what hazards may be presented.

9. Following the receipt of the laboratory results, a project specific method statement and risk assessment must be prepared to dispose of/deal with the material. Approval will be needed from the Environment Agency and the Local Authority.

10. In the event that a serious environmental incident occurs, contact the company's manager responsible for environmental issues and advise the Environment Agency using the 24 hour emergency line - **0800 80 70 60**

Guidance note - dealing with protected species, heritage and cultural aspects

If you have uninvited guests on your premises, such as certain birds, bats, lizards etc., simply evicting them is illegal. To help you to deal with these creatures in a legally safe way, follow our guidance document.

HOW TO DEAL WITH PROTECTED SPECIES, HERITAGE AND CULTURAL ASPECTS

Although it's incredibly frustrating and often costly, evicting a creature or even its nest can land you in court. To help you to avoid this situation use our **Guidance Note - Dealing with Protected Species, Heritage and Cultural Aspects**. The document covers the requirements and consequences that must be taken into account if protected species of flora and fauna, or another significant aspect such as cultural, archaeological or architectural heritage, is encountered.

GUIDANCE NOTE -
DEALING WITH PROTECTED SPECIES, HERITAGE AND CULTURAL ASPECTS

Any development work or other activities that could impact on the cultural heritage, flora and fauna, or other aspects of the environment should be carried out in such a way as to ensure that they are controlled and that appropriate measures are adopted to protect them.

Control measures

Where species of flora or fauna protected by specific legislation are encountered, all work activities should be stopped and further guidance from the local wildlife officer or English Heritage should be sought. Any work that would disturb a protected species must comply with the relevant legislation and guidance. All such work will require a licence to be obtained from English Heritage.

A full list of all protected species can be viewed at:

http://www.naturalengland.org.uk/Images/specieslistofannex_tcm6-3714.pdf.

The following control measures are to be implemented as appropriate:

- where necessary, working sites should be fenced with a standard design hoarding or other appropriate screening to protect adjacent areas of conservation interest

- to prevent disturbance to the nests of breeding birds, development areas should be cleared outside of the bird breeding season (March-August inclusive) wherever practicable. If clearance works cannot be avoided and have to be carried during the breeding season, birds should be deterred from breeding from March onwards in the areas to be affected

- where applicable, activities that may cause excessive noise and/or vibration which could cause distress to wildlife or damage to historic structures should be limited.

Many plants and animals are protected under UK law. They include species which are quite widespread, such as badgers, bats, red squirrels, slow-worms and lizards. If protected species are discovered on, or in close proximity to, an area that may be developed or changed, the presence of such species can have a significant bearing on any planning decisions and in establishing any planning restrictions/conditions.

Different species of animal and plant are afforded different levels of protection. The level of protection can also vary throughout the year depending on issues such as migratory patterns, breeding seasons and the availability of habitats, etc.

Likewise, depending on the history of the site, additional restrictions regarding the preservation of existing building features or the need for archaeological investigations may be specified.

Companies should always discuss any potential issues with the appropriate authorities at the earliest possible opportunity. The late discovery of a protected species or an item of archaeological interest on a site can result in significant delays, disruption and additional costs beyond those originally envisaged.

If there is any doubt, companies should therefore liaise with the appropriate authorities including:

- Natural England

- English Heritage

- Historic Scotland

- Scottish Natural Heritage

- Countryside Council for Wales

- Cadw

- The Environment and Heritage Service (Northern Ireland)

- your local authority

- Environment Agency

- Defra

Chapter 10

Oil storage

Oil storage policy and procedure

Oil spills are extremely harmful to the environment, very expensive to clear up and often result in prosecutions. So storage, delivery and usage of oil needs to be managed very carefully.

LEGAL POSITION

The Control of Pollution (Oil Storage) (England) Regulations 2001(CPOR), is the main piece of legislation that governs oil storage. It applies to commercial businesses who store more than 200 litres of oil, fuel, diesel etc. in tanks or containers outside and above ground level. Domestic oil users are generally exempt unless they are storing 3,500 litres or more of oil or their storage tanks are in a particularly sensitive area. Those failing to comply with the requirements of the Regulations can face a fine of up to £5,000. If oil is actually spilled, the polluter could be fined up to £20,000 at a magistrates' court, in addition to having to pay the clean-up costs. The top four causes of oil and fuel pollution incidents are tank failure, pipe failure and the overfilling of storage tanks. The purpose of the CPOR is to reduce the risks associated with these incidents by ensuring that oil storage facilities are properly designed, constructed and maintained.

OIL STORAGE POLICY AND PROCEDURES

In order to demonstrate that you are complying with the requirements of the CPOR consider developing and implementing an **Oil Storage Policy and Procedures** document.

OIL STORAGE POLICY AND PROCEDURE

General statement

It is our policy to ensure that where the risk of oil pollution from our operations has been identified as a potential problem, we will ensure that all such risks are controlled and minimised where practicable. Compliance with the **Control of Pollution (Oil Storage) (England) Regulations 2001** will be achieved.

The occurrence of oil-related water pollution is on the increase and oil has a toxic and damaging effect on the environment, as even a small amount can devastate water-based flora and fauna over a wide area.

To help ensure we give due and proper consideration to our environmental management responsibilities, and to assist in the elimination of oil pollution incidents, this Policy and Procedure has been developed. All staff are expected to abide by the following Procedure and co-operate with management in the execution of this Policy.

Procedure

Deliveries

All deliveries will be supervised by a competent person capable of dealing with any spills or other incidents that may occur. The level of all storage tanks will be checked before delivery to prevent overfilling and to ensure that the product is delivered to the correct tank.

Storage

Fuel and oil storage tanks must be sited on an impervious base and within a secure bund. The base and bund must be impermeable to the substance being stored and have sufficient capacity for daily use and for the receipt of additional deliveries. Leaking, damaged or empty tanks/drums must be removed from the site immediately and disposed of via a licensed waste disposal contractor. All bowsers must be bunded to prevent any accidental spills.

All tanks and containers shall be stored in a secure, locked area, protected from vandalism, and clearly marked with the contents of the substance. To help limit the impact of any spills, all such storage areas should be located at least ten metres from any drain or watercourse, or 50m from any well or borehole.

Where large quantities of fuel or oil are to be stored on site, the above ground storage tank should be constructed to the relevant British Standard. The bund should be constructed to contain 110% of the capacity of the storage tank, or if there is more than one container, the bund must be able to contain 110% of the largest container or 25% of the total storage capacity, whichever is the greater.

All bunds should be monitored regularly for any build up of rainwater. All water within the bund must be treated as contaminated waste and should be appropriately disposed of to eliminate the potential for further pollution.

Security

All valves and trigger guns must be protected from vandalism and unauthorised use. When not in use they should be turned off and securely locked and kept within the bund. Any tanks or drums should be stored in a secure container or compound, which should be kept locked when not in use. Bowsers must also be stored within secure compounds when not in use. Drainage valves must not be fitted to drain out rainwater.

Refuelling

All mobile plant and equipment must be refuelled in designated areas on an impermeable surface and away from any drains. A spill kit should be available at all times.

Use of plant

All fuel operated plant and equipment shall be operated within strict controls, including the use of drip trays to contain any leaks or overflow etc.

Spills

Spill kits and absorbent booms shall be available on site, where a risk assessment recommends this, to ensure that in the event of a spillage the environmental impacts are kept to a minimum. In the event of a spillage occurring, this equipment shall be used to help minimise any environmental damage prior to the implementation of more comprehensive solutions. Nominated members of staff will be trained to use and deploy the spill kits in the event of an incident.

In a serious emergency, where the spill kits are to be of no use, the Environment Agency, fire service and ambulance service shall be contacted as necessary, dependent on the consequences of the spill.

Emergency spill procedures

- try to prevent the spill from entering any drains or watercourses; use mud and earth to block its flow, or sand bags, or if available, commercial absorbents/spill kits to soak up any spilt oil

- if a pollution incident has occurred, immediately notify the Environment Agency on the emergency hotline, 0800 80 70 60. Failing to notify the Environment Agency can result in not only more widespread pollution, but in significantly higher clean up costs for the company

- ensure sufficient and appropriately sized spill kits and other absorbent materials are stored near to any oil storage areas so that they are easily accessible when needed

- train all staff in what to do in the event of a spillage and how to use any oil spill equipment.

Further guidance

The following Pollution Prevention Guidelines are relevant to oil storage and can be obtained from the Environment Agency:

- PPG08 Safe storage and disposal of used of oils

- PPG26 Storage and handling of drums and intermediate bulk containers

- PPG27 Installation, decommissioning and removal of underground storage tanks.

Remember - never hose down a spillage or use detergents to disperse it.

Guidance note - oil storage

You can't store oil in any old container. It must be specifically designed for the purpose and capable of preventing the contents from getting into the ground surface.

OIL STORAGE GUIDANCE NOTE

The exact content and requirements of the **Control of Pollution (Oil Storage) (England) Regulations 2001** (CPOR) are often not fully understood, and this makes the implementation of policies and compliance with statutory requirements more difficult to achieve. We have therefore prepared a **Guidance Note - Oil Storage**, which provides a summary of the main requirements and features of the CPOR. It can be used as an aide memoir or as a training guide to advise staff on what the requirements of the Regulations are.

GUIDANCE NOTE -
OIL STORAGE

Oil is a common and highly visible form of pollution. It can be highly poisonous to fish and other wildlife and effectively smothers plant life. Two litres of oil is sufficient to contaminate and make undrinkable the volume of fresh water needed to fill an Olympic size swimming pool.

Oil spills and leaks are also one of the most common forms of pollution reported to the Environment Agency (EA) and most occurrences could easily have been prevented through the adoption of simple procedures and control measures. Many drains lead directly to rivers, streams or lakes, so allowing oil to enter these drains has the same effect as pouring it directly into the watercourse.

The most commonly encountered types of oil are diesel and central heating oil and it is an offence to cause pollution, either deliberately or accidentally with these products. Magistrates may now impose heavy fines in such cases, and this is in addition to the cost of cleaning up the pollution.

The "Oil Storage Regulations" were brought in to try and combat this environmental problem and the final part of the **Control of Pollution (Oil Storage) (England) Regulations 2001** came into force on September 1 2005. All new oil stores and existing stores posing a "significant risk" already had to comply with the Regulations, and since September 1 2005, all other oil stores must also comply.

The Regulations mean that those who store more than 200 litres of oil in tanks and containers, outside and above ground, will need to meet new strict requirements. Failure to comply with them could mean a fine of up to £5,000 and if an oil pollution incident is caused, the polluter could be fined up to £20,000 in a Magistrates' Court.

The Regulations require the owners of oil storage tanks to provide a secondary containment facility, such as a bund or drip tray to prevent oil finding its way into the ground and watercourses. Everyone who stores more than 200 litres of oil above ground at industrial, commercial or institutional sites are affected by the Regulations. The Regulations also apply if more than 3,500 litres of oil are stored at a domestic property.

The Regulations are enforced in England by the EA; they can also offer advice and guidance to help ensure that oil storage facilities comply.

The Regulations cover oil storage at a wide variety of premises including:

- factories

- shops

- offices

- hotels

- pubs

- restaurants

- schools

- churches

- village halls

- public sector buildings

- community centres and

- hospitals.

For the purposes of the Regulations, oil includes:

- petrol

- diesel

- central heating oil

- lubricating oil

- vegetable oil

- heavy oils such as bitumen

- oils used as solvents, such as paraffin or kerosene and

- waste oil.

The Regulations not only specify spill containment requirements, but they also consider the location and structural integrity etc. The following points summarise the main requirements of the Regulations:

- tanks, drums and other oil storage containers must be strong enough to store oil without leaking or bursting

- some form of secondary containment which is impermeable to oil and water, such as a bund or drip tray, must be provided to catch any oil leaking from the container or its ancillary pipework and equipment

- for containers other than drums, the secondary container must be of sufficient capacity to contain 110% of the maximum contents of the container. Where more than one container is stored, the secondary containment should be capable of storing 110% of the largest container or 25% of the total storage capacity, whichever is the greater

- for drums, the secondary containment should be able to contain 25% of their capacity

- where possible, the oil container must be positioned to avoid damage from impact or collision. If it is not possible, then the container must be provided with some form of protection, such as a barrier or bollards

- the secondary containment must not have any outlet, valve or drain to remove rainwater or spilt oil

- all valves, the sight gauge, vent pipe and other ancillary equipment must be kept (or directed) inside the secondary container

- all underground pipework should be protected from physical damage and have adequate leak detection facilities. If mechanical pipework joints have to be used, then they should be accessible for inspection.

Domestic premises

Domestic oil storage tanks up to 2,500 litres are not normally required to be bunded unless they are sited as follows:

- located within ten metres of a watercourse

- near an open drain or manhole with a loose fitting cover.

In these cases a bunded tank will need to be installed.

Polluter pays

Finally, it is important to remember that as with all forms of environmental pollution, you have a duty of care to ensure that you take all reasonable steps to prevent any pollution incidents occurring. However, if you are found to be responsible for a pollution incident that originates from your premises, you can be required to pay the full clean-up costs.

Best practice techniques for preventing oil pollution

When it comes to oil storage, things should never be left to chance; it's certainly the time to follow best practice techniques. This will minimise the likelihood of a spill in the first place, and provide you with a good defence if the worst were to happen.

TECHNIQUES FOR PREVENTING OIL POLLUTION

There are many different actions that can be taken to prevent or minimise risks associated with oil pollution. We've identified the main **Best Practice Techniques for Preventing Oil Pollution** that can be adopted and utilised to help prevent oil pollution through spills, leaks and mismanagement. By implementing the identified measures, the risks associated with a pollution event can be significantly reduced.

BEST PRACTICE TECHNIQUES
FOR PREVENTING OIL POLLUTION

The **Control of Pollution (Oil Storage) (England) Regulations 2001** cover oil stored in tanks, intermediate bulk containers (IBCs), oil drums and mobile bowsers with a capacity of more than 200 litres.

There are a number of actions that can be taken to help control and mitigate the risks associated with the storage of oil, e.g. ensuring all new storage facilities are properly sited in areas where they are less prone to being damaged by impacts and collisions with vehicles, plant and other equipment. Storage facilities should be fitted with crash barriers or other physical protection to reduce the chances of any impact damage occurring.

Oil should not be stored within ten metres of any surface waters or within 50 metres of a borehole or well. All oil containers, tank, drums and bowsers, should be stored on a base or platform which is impervious to oil to prevent any spills or leaks seeping into the ground.

Oil storage facilities should be provided with secondary containment which will normally take the form of a bund. The bund must be constructed of oil resistant materials, be impervious and have a volume of not less than 110% of the total volume of the container if it is a single container. If the bund is containing several containers then the bund should have a capacity of 25% of the total volume of oil being contained or 110% of the largest container, whichever is the greater. Bunds must be managed and be checked for integrity and also be emptied of rainwater since this reduces their designed containment capacity.

All pipes and valves should be located within the bund and the vent pipes should be directed downwards into the bund. Access to the oil should be restricted, i.e. valves should be locked for use by designated authorised personnel only. Deliveries of oil should be supervised and oil use should be monitored to ensure that volumes can be accounted and leaks identified immediately.

The following points can also help prevent pollution incidents:

- minimise the volume of waste oil stored on site to avoid the need for consent by the EA

- dispose of waste oil through a licensed waste management contractor

- arrange for waste oil to be collected and recycled on a regular basis

- do not wash substances into surface water drains or allow run-off to seep into the ground

- have drain covers readily available to use in the event of an oil spill

- when constructing external hard surface areas, such as car parks, check the regulations for spill and surface water run-off, so that oil spills can be contained

- drain all car park, delivery and road surfaces via oil interceptors prior to discharging a surface water sewer

- divert clean roof water directly to surface water points without passing through oil/grit separators or oil interceptors. This will help to prevent interceptors becoming hydraulically overloaded

- train all staff in how to prevent oil spills and the procedures required to prevent pollution of surface and ground waters if spills do occur

- provide shovels, sand, commercial spill kits and/or absorbent pads/sawdust in locations where spills or leaks of pollutants could occur and find their way into surface water drains. Ensure that spills are cleaned up immediately to prevent potential pollution

- store above ground containers in an impermeable bund on an impermeable base

- undertake regular inspections of all oil storage vessels, pipework, valves and delivery areas to ensure that no damage, leaks or spills have occurred.

Oil storage checklist

You need to keep a close eye on your oil storage. This means that you should carry out regular checks on your storage systems and any areas in which oil is being used or decanted.

CHECKING STANDARDS ARE BEING MAINTAINED

To help you carry out a brief audit of your site, or to carry out regular checks on your storage vessels, use our **Oil Storage Checklist**. It's very simple to follow, only needing "yes" or "no" answers, and can be used as part of an audit trail or environmental management system.

Tip. If you identify any potential or actual problems, these should be formally recorded and immediate action taken to prevent a spill or one occurring again. Any ground that's identified as polluted should be cleaned and treated to prevent further pollution.

OIL STORAGE CHECKLIST

General requirements	Y	N
1. Has your tank been checked for strength and integrity so that it is unlikely to burst or leak in ordinary use?	❏	❏
2. Is all of the associated pipework in good condition with no visible leaks? . .	❏	❏
3. Do you have a secondary containment system in place (such as a drip tray, bund, or other suitable system)?	❏	❏
4. Is the secondary containment system designed to hold 110% of the volume of a single tank; or if there is more than one tank, does it hold at least 110% volume of the largest tank or 25% of the total volume?	❏	❏
5. If you are using drums, do you have a drip tray capable of holding 25% of their total volume?	❏	❏
6. Is the containment system positioned so that impact damage is minimised?	❏	❏
7. Does the containment system have a base and walls that are impervious to water and oil and which are not penetrated by any valve, pipe or opening which is used for draining the system?	❏	❏
8. If any fill pipe or draw off pipe penetrates the base or walls of the containment system, has the junction of the pipe with the base or walls been sealed to prevent oil from escaping from the system?	❏	❏
9. Are all valves, filters, sight gauges, vent pipes and other ancillary equipment (other than a fill pipe or draw off pipe) situated within the containment system?	❏	❏
10. If the fill pipe is not within the containment system, has it been fitted with a drip tray to catch any oil spilled when the tank is being filled with oil?	❏	❏

Additional requirements for fixed tanks

	Y	N

1. Are sight gauges properly supported and fitted with a valve that automatically closes when not in use? . . . . ❏ ❏

2. Are fill pipes and draw off pipes positioned to minimise damage from impact? . . . . ❏ ❏

3. Has the tank been fitted with an automatic overfill prevention device if you can't see it or any vent pipe during filling?. . . . . ❏ ❏

4. Is the screw fitting or other fixed coupling in good condition and in use when the tank is being filled? . . . . ❏ ❏

5. Where oil is delivered from the tank through a permanently attached flexible pipe:

   • Does the pipe, at the delivery end, have a tap or valve fitted that closes automatically when not in use?. . . . . ❏ ❏

   • Is the tap or valve not capable of being fixed in the open position unless the pipe has been fitted with an automatic shut off device?. . . . . . ❏ ❏

   • When not in use is the delivery pipe kept in a secure cabinet that is kept locked shut and equipped with a drip tray? . . . . ❏ ❏

   • If the delivery pipe is not in a cabinet does it have a lockable valve that is kept locked shut and which is located within the containment system?. . . . . ❏ ❏

6. Where a pump is fitted:

   • Is it fitted with a non-return valve in its feed line?. . . . . ❏ ❏

   • Is it positioned so as to minimise damage from impact? . . . . ❏ ❏

   • Is it protected from unauthorised use? . . . . ❏ ❏

7. Are permanent vent pipes, taps or valves through which oil can discharge:

   • Within the containment system? . . . . ❏ ❏

   • Arranged so as to discharge oil vertically downwards? . . . . ❏ ❏

   • In the case of a tap or valve, fitted with a lock and kept locked shut when not in use?. . . . . ❏ ❏

Guidance note - pollution response plan

Although you should have done your best to prevent a spill, one may still occur. However, quick and efficient action can minimise the impact and save you the cost of a clean up operation or even prosecution.

POLLUTION RESPONSE PLAN

Even if you don't have an environmental permit, which requires you to have a pollution response plan, it's still worth having one if you store hazardous substances, e.g. oil. Having a plan for responding to leaks and spills ensures that your staff have the right information to hand in the event of an emergency. Our **Guidance Note - Pollution Response Plan** includes an outline of the information to include in your emergency procedure. By following our guide you will have pulled together all the essential information you need in the event of a spill including plans of the site, emergency contacts and details of spillage materials.

GUIDANCE NOTE -
POLLUTION RESPONSE PLAN

Most industrial, commercial and construction sites have the potential to cause significant environmental harm through spills and leaks of oil and other hazardous substances. But such incidents need not result in serious environmental damage provided that appropriate pollution prevention measures are immediately put in place.

This guidance note will help you to develop a pollution incident response plan. You must have such a plan if you have an environmental permit (England and Wales), a pollution prevention and control (PPC) permit (Northern Ireland and Scotland) or are regulated by the Control of Major Accident Hazards (COMAH) Regulations. Whilst not all businesses are subject to these legal requirements, developing these contingency arrangements will make you better prepared to prevent a pollution incident on your site. In any case, pollution incidents can result in expensive clean-up operations and are therefore worth avoiding.

What is a pollution incident response plan?

A pollution incident response plan is a short document that outlines the actions your business will take to minimise the risk of pollution in the event of an incident, such as an oil leak.

What information should your pollution incident response plan contain?

The following is an outline of the information to include in your plan:

Introduction

- the date the plan was produced and when it is due for review
- the **name** of your business
- your **address** and the location of your premises or site and a description of the surrounding area
- the manager with overall responsibility for the plan
- the person responsible for keeping the plan up-to-date
- a list of the **operations** that take place on your premises, particularly those with the potential to cause environmental damage
- the number of employees present at different times of the day
- the arrangements for briefing staff including new starters and temporary workers, who could be involved in responding to an incident.

Key contact details

List 24-hour contact details for people and organisations that may need to be involved during or after a pollution incident. For example:

- staff who are responsible for making decisions and taking action in the event of a spill or leak
- the most **senior** responsible person (who should be informed of the incident immediately)
- the emergency services, your environmental regulator, the Health and Safety Executive and the pollution hotline (0800 80 70 60)
- your **water company or authority** and sewerage undertaker if different
- local GP surgeries and hospitals with accident and emergency departments
- specialist clean-up contractors.

Detailing pollution risks and other relevant facillities at your site

Include a detailed site plan that shows **areas vulnerable to pollution**, including the locations of storage and delivery areas, any other areas that could cause pollution, and locations of surface watercourses, culverts and porous or unmade ground that could be affected by a pollution incident. Include on the plan buildings, access routes for emergency services, on-site water treatment facilities (if applicable), volumes of tanks, or drum store areas, bunds including retention capacity, mains stop cock, sprinkler control valves (where applicable, hydrants and pollution prevention materials. Also include oil separators and other devices which may be useful in controlling pollution, e.g. drain shut-off valves.

Draw a schematic plan of the site drainage arrangements using red lines for foul and blue lines for surface water drainage. Indicate the direction of flow. Show the location of soak-aways and note their depth and construction details. If there is a delay in producing this, as an interim measure at least mark the drain covers etc. on a plan and indicate whether they are foul or surface water. You should also find out whether your site is in a ground water source protection zone and check the implications for your activities.

Note the sewage works which receives your foul waste and find out from the water undertaker, the nearest foul sewer pumping station serving your site. (By being able to give clear information to the water company representative in the event of an emergency, they will then know which pumping station could be turned off in order to prevent the pollution being carried to the treatment works).

List the types of **fuel, oils, gases and chemicals** you store on your site. Include estimates of how much of these you normally keep on site to help the emergency services in an incident. Attach product data sheets and COSHH (control of substances hazardous to health) assessments for any substances that pose a risk to people or the environment.

How to deal with pollution incidents

Your pollution prevention plan should describe the **actions** to take in the event of an incident and who is **responsible** for them.

The plan should contain details of how to:

- **stop** incidents occurring, e.g. prevent leaks

- **contain** incidents, e.g. how to use spill kits, drain blockers and other devices to prevent spilled materials entering drains or watercourses: include a list of all materials and equipment held on site to deal with pollution, substances posing a particular risk and means of making leaking containers safe

- **notify** relevant contacts when an incident occurs, e.g. key staff, environmental regulators, nearby property owners who may need to be alerted (e.g. if they are vulnerable to pollution) and emergency services

- **clean up** after any incident, e.g. how you will store and dispose of contaminated materials, protective clothing and equipment, plus details of specialist contractors and when to use them.

- **investigate and put in place improvements to prevent a recurrence.**

Guidance note - oil separators

In accordance with Environment Agency guidance, oil separators (or interceptors) should be installed on surface water drainage systems where the potential exists for pollution such as oil, diesel and petrol to enter your drainage system.

OIL SEPARATORS

Our **Guidance Note - Oil Separators** details the different types of separator, where they should be used and the type of information needed in order to design and select the appropriate interceptor for any given situation.

GUIDANCE NOTE -
OIL SEPARATORS

In accordance with Environment Agency guidance, oil separators (or interceptors) should be installed on surface water drainage systems where the potential exists for pollutants such as oil, diesel and petrol to enter the drainage system and be discharged into either a watercourse or the public drainage network.

The type and size of separator required for any given situation will depend on a number factors including:

- the type of pollutants entering the drainage system
- the toxicity of the pollutant
- the maximum anticipated volume of fuel/diesel/oil expected to pass through the interceptor
- the anticipated flow and volume of surface water to pass through the interceptor
- the sensitivity of the receiving watercourse
- the location of the interceptor
- the maintenance and inspection regime
- any environmental agency requirements.

Most separators are prefabricated glass reinforced plastic structures that are buried beneath the ground at the downstream end of the drainage system. Separators should conform to BS EN 858-1:2002. They function by passing the flow of water through a series of baffles within the tank - this has the effect of retaining fuel, diesel and oils which are separated and retained. The contaminated material can then be removed by tanker for disposal at a licensed waste disposal site. There are a number of specialist suppliers of separators who can supply a variety of sizes to cater for most circumstances.

There are four principal types of separator, and each is summarised below.

Full retention separator:

- suitable for high risk sites
- available in Class 1 and Class 2 formats
- separates oil spills
- all surface water is treated
- can discharge to surface water drainage systems
- capable of handling flow rates up to 200 litres per second.

Bypass separator:

- suitable for lower risk sites such as car parks
- available in Class 1 and Class 2 formats
- capable of treating peak flows in excess of 1,000 litres per second
- can discharge to surface water drainage.

Wash down separator:

- used in applications such as car wash facilities and construction site wash down areas
- generally discharges to a foul sewer.

Forecourt separator:

- designed to capture 7,600 litres of spillage from one cell of a fuel delivery tanker
- available in Class 1 and 2 formats.

  Class 1 separators are designed to achieve a discharge concentration of less than 5 mg/litre of oil under standard test conditions. These separators are required for discharges to surface water drains and the water environment. Many Class 1 separators contain coalescing devices, which draw the oil droplets together and facilitate the separation.

  Class 2 separators are designed to achieve a discharge concentration of less than 100 mg/litre of oil under standard test conditions. They are suitable for dealing with discharges where a lower quality requirement applies such as discharges to the foul sewer.

Further detailed information is provided in the Environment Agency's Pollution Prevention Guideline No. 3. (PPG 3) **Use and design of oil separators in surface water drainage systems**. This can be downloaded from the following website:

http://publications.environment-agency.gov.uk/pdf/PMHO0406BIYL-e-e.pdf?lang=e.

<u>Glossary of key environmental terms</u>

Glossary of key environmental terms

BAT: Best Available Techniques, defined under Integrated Pollution Prevention and Control (IPPC). Note that BAT has many more cost and implementation issues than its predecessor BATNEEC.

BATNEEC: Best Available Techniques Not Entailing Excessive Cost, defined under Integrated Pollution Control (IPC).

Biodiversity: The range of plant and animal species and communities associated with terrestrial, aquatic and marine habitats.

Biological treatment: Any biological process that changes the properties of waste (for example, anaerobic digestion, composting). Biological treatment includes land spreading activities that are licensed.

BPEO: Best Practicable Environmental Option, a procedure that takes into account the total impact of a process and the technical possibilities for dealing with it. BPEO establishes the waste management option, or mix of options, that provides the most benefits or the least damage to the environment as a whole, at acceptable cost, in the long-term as well as in the short-term.

Climate Change Levy: A tax introduced on April 1 2001, which is designed to stimulate business improvements in energy efficiency.

Controlled waste: The UK term for wastes controlled under the Waste Framework Directive: any household, industrial or commercial waste.

Defra: Department for Environment, Food and Rural Affairs.

Eco-efficiency: The delivery of competitively priced goods and services that satisfy human needs and bring quality of life, while progressively reducing environmental impacts and resource intensity throughout the life cycle, to a level at least in line with the earth's estimated carrying capacity.

ELV(s): End of Life Vehicle - scrap cars and other vehicles. The subject of an EU Directive.

EMAS: (European) Eco-management and Audit Scheme. A European voluntary scheme for industrial sites. To register under EMAS your company should have a clearly defined strategy for environmental management, complete with quantified objectives.

EMS: Environmental Management Systems: the part of an overall management system that includes organisational structure, planning activities, responsibilities, practices, procedures, processes and procedures for developing, implementing, achieving, reviewing and maintaining the environmental policy (see ISO 14001).

Energy recovery: The recovery of useful energy in the form of heat and/or power from burning waste. Generally applied to incineration, but can also include the combustion of landfill gas and gas produced during anaerobic digestion.

Environment Agency: The principal environmental regulator in England and Wales. Established in April 1996 to combine the functions of former waste regulation authorities, the National Rivers Authority and Her Majesty's Inspectorate of Pollution. Intended to promote improved waste management and consistency in waste regulation across England and Wales.

Environmental accounting: Any quantitative approach to linking financial and environmental performance.

Environmental footprint: The impact of an organisation in environmental terms (resource use, waste generation, physical environmental changes etc).

Environmental Technology Best Practice Programme (ETBPP): A Government (DEFRA) initiative to demonstrate the benefits of reducing resource use and environmental impact to companies across the whole of the UK.

EU Directive: A European Union legal instruction, binding on all Member States but which must be implemented through national legislation within a prescribed time-scale.

Exempt facility: A waste recovery operation (also occasionally certain disposal at the waste producer and some storage activities) registered with, but not licensed by, the Environment Agency. Exempt facilities are subject to general rules (e.g. on the types and quantities of wastes received).

Hazardous waste: Defined by EU legislation as the most harmful wastes to people and the environment. Hazardous wastes are listed in the List of Wastes (England) Regulations 2005.

Fauna: The collective term for animal life.

Flora: The collective term for plant life.

Incineration: The burning of waste at high temperatures in the presence of sufficient air to achieve complete combustion, either to reduce its volume (in the case of municipal solid waste) or its toxicity (for example, for organic solvents). Municipal solid waste incinerators recover heat and/or power. The main emissions are carbon dioxide, water and ash residues.

Industrial waste: Waste from any factory or industrial process (excluding mines and quarries).

Inert waste: Chemically inert, non-combustible, non-biodegradable and non-polluting waste defined in the EU Directive on the Landfill of Waste.

IPC: Integrated Pollution Control, a system introduced under the Environmental Protection Act 1990, which controls polluting substances from industrial processes to the three environmental media of air, land and water. IPC was designed to ensure that best available techniques not entailing excessive costs are used to prevent, or where that is not practicable, to reduce, emissions from a range of the potentially most polluting industrial processes, including some waste management facilities. Gradually being replaced with Pollution, Prevention and Control requirements under the EU IPPC Directive.

IPPC: Integrated Pollution Prevention and Control, an EC Directive implemented in the UK by the Pollution Prevention and Control (England and Wales) Regulations 2000. This is similar to IPC but also covers noise, vibration, resource minimisation, energy efficiency, environmental accidents and site protection and covers more industrial processes.

ISO 14001: An environmental management system (EMS) is a systematic approach to dealing with the environmental impacts of an organisation. It is a framework that enables an organisation of any size or type to control the impact of its activities, products or services on the natural environment. ISO 14001 is an international standard that specifies the requirements.

Landfill (sites): Licensed facilities where waste is permanently deposited for disposal.

Landfill tax: A tax that applies to active and inert waste, disposed at a licensed landfill. The aim of the tax is to send a tough signal to waste managers to switch to less environmentally damaging alternatives to disposal.

Land spreading: Recovering waste by spreading onto land principally for agricultural benefit or ecological improvement. Sewage sludge and wastes from, for example, the food, brewing and paper pulp industries can be used for this purpose.

LFD: Landfill Directive

Licensed site/waste management facility: A waste disposal or recovery facility licensed under the Environmental Protection Act.

Life Cycle Analysis (Assessment): LCA is a systematic technique for identifying and evaluating the potential environmental benefits and impacts (use of resources; human health; ecological consequences) associated with a product or function throughout its entire life from extraction of raw materials to its eventual disposal and assimilation into the environment. LCA helps to place the assessment of the environmental costs and benefits of these various options, and the development of appropriate and practical waste management policies, on a sound and objective basis.

Pollution incidents:

- Category 1: incidents having persistent and extensive impact on land, air or water.
- Category 2: incidents having significant impact on land, air or water.
- Category 3: incidents having minimal impact on land, air or water.

Process Mapping: A logical step by step representation of business activities showing key inputs/outputs.

Producer responsibility: Requires industry and commerce involved in the manufacture, distribution and sale of particular goods to take greater responsibility for the disposal and/or recovery of those goods at the end of their useful life.

Recovery: Involves the recovery of value from waste, through recycling, composting or incineration with energy recovery.

Recycling: Involves the reprocessing of wastes, either into the same material (closed-loop) or a different material (open-loop recycling). Commonly applied to non-hazardous wastes such as paper, glass, cardboard, plastics and metals. However, hazardous wastes (such as solvents) can also be recycled by specialist companies, or using in-house equipment.

Reduction: Reducing the quantity or the hazard of a waste produced from a process. It usually results in reduced raw material and energy demands - thus also reducing costs.

Re-use: Using materials or products again, for the same or a different purpose, without material reprocessing (such as glass milk bottles or returnable plastic crates).

Sustainable development: Development which meets the needs of the present without compromising the ability of future generations to meet their own needs.

Sustainable waste management: Using material resources efficiently to cut down on the amount of waste produced. And, where waste is generated, dealing with it in a way that actively contributes to the economic, social and environmental goals of sustainable development.

TCOW: True Cost of Waste. The cost of waste is always much greater than just the cost of disposal, and can be as much as 5-10% of a company's turnover. Waste disposal is the obvious "visible" cost but there are numerous hidden costs.

Treatment: Involves the physical, chemical or biological processing of waste to reduce their volume or harmfulness.

Waste hierarchy: The ranking of waste management options in order of sustainability.

Waste management: Management of the collection, recovery and disposal of wastes, including options for waste reduction.

Waste minimisation: The reduction of waste at source, by understanding and changing processes to reduce and prevent waste. This is also known as process or resource efficiency. Waste minimisation can include the substitution of less environmentally harmful materials in the production process.